The Nature Corner

M. v. Leeuwen and J. Moeskops

The Nature Corner

Celebrating the year's cycle with seasonal tableaux

Floris Books

Translated by Polly Lawson
Photographs by Frits Dijkhof
Illustrations by Ronald Heuninck

First published in Dutch as *De Seizoenentafel* by Christofoor Publishers in 1990
First published in English in 1990 by Floris Books, Edinburgh
Second edition 2008
Second printing 2015

British Library CIP data available

ISBN 978-086315-646-5

Printed in Malaysia

Contents

Introduction

A seasonal tableau or seasons' table is a place in the home where you can follow the natural cycle of the year. Changes which are taking place in the natural world are given expression indoors. The figures on the seasons' table depict the essence of what is happening in nature. Creating and maintaining the seasonal tableau will sharpen your observation of what goes on in nature. Looking after the table can be absorbing, and you will always be on the look out for suitable items to represent each season.

This search enables us to live in accordance with the rhythm of the spring equinox, summer solstice, autumn equinox, midwinter, and so on. We are no longer simply swept along by the passage of time but consciously experience the rhythm of the year. This can be a great source of security.

Young children do not knowingly study nature, but they are nevertheless unconsciously aware of its laws. When we bring the external world indoors, creating a seasonal table in colours without the use of words, children learn to appreciate the many ways in which nature is at work in their surroundings.

Older children can help to collect beautiful natural objects for the seasonal tableau. Often they will make something themselves which is worthy of a place.

Adults and older children are less likely to use dolls in their creation; a vase with branches or flowers of the season, a print or a beautiful stone is often sufficient.

All that is needed to create a seasonal tableau is somewhere to put the items, such as a special table or shelf set apart in the home. It is best if this particular place does not change; this will give children a constant focus for their attention.

Arranging a seasonal tableau

The basic element of a seasonal tableau is some soft flowing material such as velvet, wool-cotton mix, or silk, cut to appropriate size. The fabric can simply be laid on the table, or it can also serve as a background, in which case lift one corner up and tie it to a fixture higher up, varying the height of the background according to the tableau.

The sky can be made from a piece of material with a broad hem along one side. Push a length of wire through the hem and bend it to make a semicircle. Tie string to each end and pull tightly to hold the bow in shape (Figure 1).

Place solid objects under the cloth to make areas of different heights for displaying different items.

The colours of the ground and background are very important because they express the mood of the season (compare the photos of the various seasons' tables in this book). The colour circle (Figure 2) can be of help here.

Stones, round logs and vases of various sizes are also useful items.

The southern hemisphere

In the southern hemisphere the date of Christmas falls at the summer solstice — in the middle of summer. To follow the suggestions in this book, in order to recreate a northern hemisphere mood, would be disruptive.

It is a particular challenge in these parts of the world to find a way of celebrating the festivals

Figure 1. Wire threaded through hem; tie the ends of the string behind the cloth

while reflecting the nature of the seasons in the region. We hope that this book stimulates your own imagination and creativity, so that appropriate tableaux can be created which combine the local seasonal character with the universal timing of the festivals.

Using the seasons' table

The seasonal tableaux in this book reflect particular moments in the year. They were created specially for this book. In your home the seasonal tableau will look different because it will always be changing, with objects coming and going.

Children should be allowed to touch and move the objects on a seasonal table, although generally these are not meant to be taken from the table and played with. In our home Mary and Joseph move towards the stable and arrive there at Christmas — a helpful contribution from the children.

There are many figures which you will want to make. Mother Earth, for example, is a central figure, and she can be present all the year round. Of course, bought items can also be placed on the seasonal table — for example wooden animals, plaster crib figures, chocolate Easter hares, eggs, cut crystal, a candlestick, a postcard or a print. Flowers should be changed regularly, as this also shows the changing of the seasons.

At all times the tableau should be appropriate to the particular season, and the particular children. For young children it can be dressed much more simply than described in this book.

A tableau could also be based on a book relevant to a particular season; in winter, for example, you could use Elsa Beskow's picture book, *Ollie's*

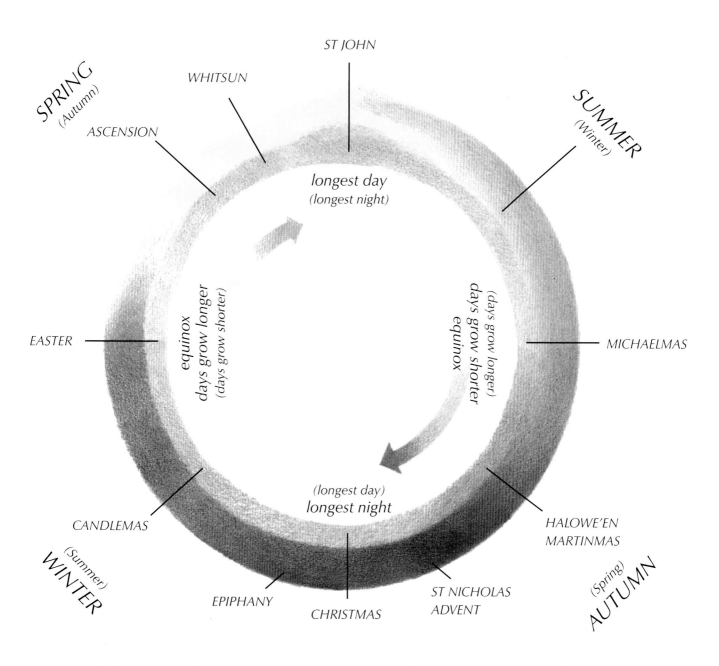

ST JOHN

WHITSUN

SPRING
(Autumn)

SUMMER
(Winter)

ASCENSION

longest day
(longest night)

EASTER

equinox
days grow longer
(days grow shorter)

(days grow longer)
days grow shorter
equinox

MICHAELMAS

(longest day)
longest night

CANDLEMAS

HALOWE'EN
MARTINMAS

(Summer)
WINTER

ST NICHOLAS
ADVENT

(Spring)
AUTUMN

EPIPHANY

CHRISTMAS

Figure 2. Colour circle of the year   *(The seasons of the southern hemisphere)*

Ski Trip (see Further reading at the end of the book).

A seasonal tableau is an excellent tool to help celebrate of the year's festivals. (Suggestions for further reading on the meaning of the festivals can also be found at the back of the book.)

Becoming more acquainted with the meaning of the festivals will help you to find the right things for the seasonal tableau.

You will discover that the results can vary a lot. Trying to improve and adapt the tableau is an ongoing — and fun! — challenge.

1. Basic techniques

The dolls in this book are made using various techniques which we shall describe briefly. Of course you can choose any technique for any doll; for example the Spring Fairy can be made on a stand, or the Christmas group can also be made of teased sheep's wool.

Doll made with sheep's wool

Well-teased unspun sheep's wool is gently pulled and shaped. The head is formed by making a knot in the wool. This technique is suitable for making figures with less definition (see also Saint Nicholas on page 66).

Marionette

A marionette has a shaped head (see below). The body is formed from the material projecting from the head. Insert a marble or a little stone inside the base of the body to ensure that the marionette hangs vertically. The clothing is loose. Usually the marionette is hung on a wire (see also the Spring Fairy on page 25).

Standing doll

This doll's head is made with knitted cotton (see page 13). The body is formed by firmly stuffing the dress which can be knitted, crocheted, or

Figure 3. Doll made with sheep's wool

Figure 4. Marionette

Figure 5. Doll on a cardboard cone

Doll on a cardboard cone

This doll's head is also made from knitted cotton. The body is made from a semicircular piece of cardboard bent round to form a cone with a hole for the neck. The arms are made of wire or pipe-cleaners. The clothing is draped on to the figure (Figure 5).

This technique is only suitable for rather shapeless dolls. It is used for the Christmas crib figures for instance, where too much characterization is inappropriate.

Doll on a stand

A doll with a slender figure can have a head (see page 13) set on a wooden stand. The stand is made from a round disc of wood or plywood about 2 in (5 cm) in diameter, and a piece of dowelling as thick as a pencil and of the requisite length. Bore a hole in the middle of the disc and glue in the dowelling. Sharpen the other end. About 2 in (5 cm) below the point bore a tiny hole in the stick. This hole is used when fixing the head (Figure 6).

The arms are made of wire bound round with wool. Sew them on at the back. This doll can have clothes made to measure. The doll's figure will depend on how much wool is worked in under the clothing (see also Mother Earth on page 19).

Doll made of wire

This doll also has a formed head (see page 13). If the doll is to have proper legs and feet, the frame should be made of wire or pipe-cleaner. Wire can

made of felt. The stuffing is sheep's wool (see also the flower children on page 27).

If the doll will not stand up securely, there is an easy way to stabilize it. Cut out a disc of cardboard and a disc of felt of the same colour and circumference as the bottom of the dress, place the cardboard disc inside the bottom of the dress and sew the felt piece over it on to the edge of the dress.

If necessary the doll can be stabilized further by inserting something heavy, such as a marble or pebbles, before sewing it up.

Figure 8. Shoes made of lead flashing

Figure 6. Doll on a stand

Figure 7. Doll made of wire

be bent more often than pipe-cleaner, but it is not so easily worked (Figure 7).

The shoes can be made of moulded beeswax. However, the doll can easily topple over if it is not stuck to a flat base. To prevent this you could use lead flashing to line the shoes (Figure 8). Lead flashing is thin lead used in roofing which can be cut with scissors.

The shoes are made of two layers of lead flashing, the bottom layer forming the sole. Make a hole in the upper layer with a nail and push the wire of the foot through so that the end of the wire lies between the two layers of lead flashing. Pull a piece of knitted cotton or felt tightly over the lead to make the shoes and tie it up round the ankle. (Do not use lead where there are young children, as lead is toxic.)

A doll made of wire can be bent into any posture desired (see also the Whitsun bride on page 40).

Making a doll's head

The head for most of these dolls is made in the following way.

Make a ball by stuffing some clean, teased sheep's wool into a piece of soft thin knitted cotton. Leave some wool sticking out at the neck. Head size is indicated in the pattern, the measurements

13

Figures 9–12. Measuring the doll's head. Tying the head. The eye line. The chin thread.

being taken over the head, from one side of the neck to the other (Figure 9).

Tie up the neck firmly using strong thread such as embroidery thread. This we shall call tying-up thread. A slip-knot is tied as follows: wind a thread loosely twice round the neck, pass the right end under the left, pass it under both threads and pull tight and tie a knot (Figure 10). With a needle take the ends of the thread right through the head (coming out anywhere) and cut them off close to the material, so the ends are now hidden inside the wool.

To form the **eye line**, tie a thread around the middle of the ball with the same knot used for tying up the neck. Before knotting, check that the thread is located correctly in the middle of the ball and is sufficiently tight to make a depression but not to divide the ball into two parts. Leave the ends of the thread uncut (Figure 11).

Choose the side best suited for the face, bearing in mind where the cheeks and chin are to go, then ease the knot in the thread on the eye line round to the side (the ear point).

Once the eye line has been positioned make a cross-stitch on the ear point with the ends from the knot. Stick the needle right through the head to the other ear point, pull the thread fairly tight and make another cross-stitch. Now pass the threads right through the head and cut the ends off. At the back of the head bring the eye line thread down to the neck to shape the back of the head.

Making a **chin thread** will give the head even more definition. Make a head as in Figure 11. The longer of the two threads hanging down from the knot on the eye line is called the working thread. Bring this under the chin and back up to the eye line, pass it under the eye thread and pull it tight, then take it over the middle of the head again back to the first ear point. Tie the working thread firmly to the hanging thread at the ear

Figures 13–15. Making a nose. Tube of knitted cotton. Finishing the head.

point. Thread the longer of the two threads and stitch two crosses on top of each other over the ear point. Pass the needle right through the head to a point exactly opposite. Pull the thread tight so the head becomes slightly oval and work two cross-stitches over each other. Tease the eye line at the back of the head down to the base of the head (Figure 12). All the threads are then passed right through the head and cut off.

If the features of the face are to be marked you can make a **nose**. Sew a little lump of wool or a small bead in the middle of the face just below the eye line. Check the appearance by covering it with a piece of thicker knitted cotton, as you will do to finish the head.

An older face needs a drawn-in **mouth**. Stick a pin in to mark the position of the mouth. Using strong thread push a long needle in at the corner of the mouth right through the head. Pull the thread

out of the needle and rethread the end hanging at the front. Push the needle in again at the other corner of the mouth right through the head. Pull the two ends tight, at the same time checking the front to see that it looks right. Tie the threads together at the back of the head. Pass the ends through the head and cut them off. If the face is to look older still, use the same technique to create lines running down from the side of the nose past the corners of the mouth and down by the chin (Figure 13).

Once the inside of the head is finished, cover the head with thicker skin-coloured knitted cotton. As not all knitted cotton is equally elastic it is not possible to give exact measurements in the patterns. The rib runs vertically over the head. Measure out a piece which fits tightly around the head in width and is twice as long as the head. Sew this piece into a tube (Figure 14). Turn it inside out and draw it over the head so that at the top there is just enough material to cover the head. Tie a strong thread round the neck. Cut the cloth on the top of the head so that it forms strips which you can lay the flat on the head and sew on securely (Figure 15).

With very small dolls it is not necessary to make an inner head. Instead, make a little tube of thick knitted cotton (Figure 14), sew across one end and draw tight to close it. Turn the bag inside out and fill with wool. Tie up the neck. Be careful to preserve the proportion of the head to the body.

Finishing off the face

To mark the position of the **eyes**, stick pins in on the eye line. See if the doll is looking at you! The **mouth** forms an inverted equilateral triangle with the eyes. Stick a pin in here too. With a coloured pencil draw dots in place of the pins.

The eyes will be more accentuated if you make a depression in the following way. Mark the place of the eyes with pins. Thread a long needle with strong thread. Push the needle into the corner of the eye beside the pin and push it right through the head to the back and pull it through. Unthread the needle. Thread the needle with the thread hanging at the front. Remove the pin. Decide on the width of the eye and insert the needle once again right through the head from the eye line and pull it through. Form the other eye in the same way. Tighten the four threads and check the effect. Tie the threads but be careful not to pull too hard in case the eyes are too deep. Rethread the ends through the head and cut them off.

Now the face can be coloured. You can make rosy **cheeks** by brushing them on using a cloth covered in wax crayon, but be careful not to overdo the effect.

Hair

There are several ways in which you can give your dolls some hair.

Hair from unspun sheep's wool

White, brown, grey, black or natural wool, or "magic wool" which is washed and carded dyed wool, can be used. Place a little tuft of wool on the head and shape it into a hairstyle. With small stitches sew the wool firmly on to the head using thread of the same colour.

Embroidered hair

Use knitting wool, embroidery wool, darning wool, embroidery thread, mohair, cotton or silk thread.

Decide where the crown of the head is to be and make the first stitch which is a long stitch over the head towards the forehead. Now make a little stitch under the material, and then a long stitch back up to the top again. This second stitch must be a little shorter than the first, otherwise the crown of the head will become too thick. Stitch down to the back of the head and back up again to the top, then down to the ears and back up again (Figure 16). Now the head is divided into four parts. Divide each of these parts into two by stitching down and up in the same manner, and continue in this way until the whole head is filled.

Finally you can finish off with a fringe or long hair for a ponytail or plaits between the stitched hair.

Figure 16. Embroidered hair

2. Early spring

Before spring nature still seems to be at rest, but under the surface of the earth there is much activity. This only becomes visible in the early spring when flowers such as crocuses, hyacinths and narcissi thrust up through the earth seeking the light.

Children will be made more aware of this if you make Mother Earth and her root children for the seasonal tableau, and tell the story of how Mother Earth wakes them and sets them to work. For weeks the root children dye and sew their new clothes which must be ready as soon as spring comes. The eager little snowdrop cannot wait and only has time to give her green tassel a little dusting. The daisy who has pricked her finger in the difficult work of cutting and sewing takes care that drops of blood fall only on the underside of the petals.

Mother Earth not only looks after flowers and plants, she also cares for us: she gives us food and sustains us.

Mother Earth

MATERIALS

A piece of soft thin knitted cotton 6 in x 6 in (15 x 15 cm)

Wool

A piece of salmon-coloured thicker knitted cotton 3 1/2 in x 4 in (8.5 x 10 cm)

A wooden stand 6 in (15 cm) high (see page 13)

Wire 16 in (40 cm) long, 1/32 in (0.8 mm) thick

A scrap of thicker knitted cotton for the hands

Grey unspun wool for the hair

For her clothes you will need material in varying shades of earthy colours:

A round piece of soft cloth 10 1/2 in (26.5 cm) diameter for the petticoat

A piece of cloth 8 3/4 in x 6 1/4 in (22 x 16 cm) for the blouse

A piece of cloth 15 in x 5 1/2 in (38 x 14 cm) for the skirt

A piece of cloth 4 1/4 in x 4 1/4 in (11 x 11 cm) and a tape 8 3/4 in x 1 1/4 in (22 x 3 cm) for the apron

A round piece of cloth 4 1/4 in (11 cm) diameter for the bonnet, or alternatively a piece of cloth 6 in x 4 1/4 in (15 x 11 cm) and a tape of 2 1/4 in x 3/4 in (6 x 2 cm) for a little cap

A scrap of knitted wool for a shawl

A piece of cloth 16 in x 8 in (40 x 20 cm) for a cloak

A piece of cloth 7 in x 7 in (18 x 18 cm) of the same colour as the cloak for the hood

12 in (30 cm) bias binding of the same colour as the cloak

Possibly a piece of very thin wire for the spectacles

A basket

METHOD

Make a 4 3/4 in (12 cm) head of knitted cotton. This measurement is taken over the head from one side of the neck to the other (see page 13).

Mother Earth has a very old face, and so she should be given a nose, and lines round her mouth. After covering the head with thicker knitted cotton the eyes and the mouth can be indented.

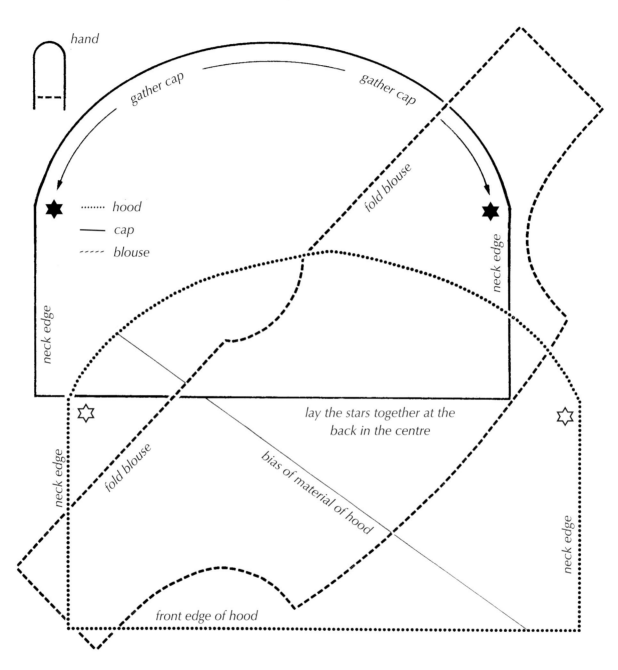

hand

gather cap

gather cap

fold blouse

.... hood
——— cap
- - - - blouse

neck edge

neck edge

fold blouse

neck edge

bias of material of hood

lay the stars together at the
back in the centre

neck edge

front edge of hood

Figure 17. Pattern for Mother Earth

Place the head on the stand (see page 13) and tie it on to the stick with the bits of material hanging down from the head. Pass the thread two or three times through the hole in the stand, so that the head is secured. Check the overall height, which must be 7 in (18 cm).

Make the arms by bending the two ends of the wire back to the middle to make a piece 7 in (18 cm) long. Sew the middle of the wire firmly to the back about $1/2$ in (1 cm) below the head.

Bind the arms with sheep's wool to fill them out. Mould Mother Earth's bosom with wool too. If the wool will not stay in place it can be secured with a few stitches.

Draw the hands as shown in the pattern (Figure 17) on a double thickness of material and sew together on the line. Cut the hands out leaving a small seam and turn them. Pull the hands over the ends of the arms and secure them to the wrists.

Cut out the petticoat. Tack round $1/2$ in (1 cm) from the edge. Place the stand in the middle of the material and draw up the tacking thread, gathering the petticoat around the dowelling at waist height. Secure.

Cut out the blouse according to the pattern (Figure 17) adding a small seam allowance. Sew together and cut an opening in the middle of the back. Put the blouse on. Gather the sleeves firmly round the wrists and sew up the slit at the back. Gather the edge of the neck and secure with little stitches.

Cut out the skirt according to the measurements given and hem the bottom edge. Sew up the back. Turn the raw edge to the inside and tack a double thread around the top of the skirt. Pull the skirt on over the blouse, pull in the tacking thread and secure.

Hem the apron at the sides and bottom. Gather the top. Lay the mid-point of the tape to the mid-point of the apron and sew it on along the top of the apron.

Fold the tape over, turn it in and hem the whole tape. Mother Earth wears her apron for work.

Make the hair with grey sheep's wool (see page 17). Make a parting in the middle by fixing the wool with little embroidery stitches. You can make a bun at the back of her head by twisting the wool and stitching it down.

Now Mother Earth is ready for a cap or bonnet on her head. Cut out the material for the cap according to the pattern (Figure 17). Hem the straight edge which now becomes the front. Tack the round edge and gather this in to the width of the tape 2 $1/2$ in (6 cm). Sew the tape on to the gathers on the right side of the cap. Fold the tape over and hem it on.

For the bonnet hem round the piece of cloth. Run a doubled length of gathering thread $1/4$ in (7 mm) from the edge. Pull in the gathering thread a little, put the bonnet on the head and pull in the gathering thread more if necessary. Spread the folds evenly over the bonnet and set it firmly on the head.

For a knitted shawl use 3 mm needles.
Cast on 50 stitches.
Knit in moss-stitch for 18 rows, (that is, 1 purl, 1 plain on each row alternately), decreasing 1 stitch at the beginning of each row.

Now decrease one stitch at each end 10 times.
12 stitches remain.
Decrease 3 stitches 4 times.

The shawl is now about 8 in (20 cm) wide and 2 3/4 in (7 cm) at its longest point.

For a crochet shawl make a chain to a length of 8 in (20 cm). Then make alternately treble and single crochets in continuously decreasing rows so that a piece is made of the same measurements as those of the knitted shawl.

For a sewn shawl select a loosely woven material which will drape nicely round the little shoulders. Cut out a piece of the same measurements as the knitted shawl. Hem the shawl all round.

Finally attach a fringe to the diagonal edge of whichever type of shawl you have made. In cold weather Mother Earth can wear her shawl.

When it grows colder Mother Earth wears a cloak in which she can wrap herself completely. Cut out the cloak according to the measurements given. Hem the sides and bottom, and gather the top.

Cut out the hood according to the pattern (Figure 17) with a small seam allowance, noting the direction of the bias. Hem the long straight edge. Lay the neck edges together and sew up the round edge.

Lay the gathered edge of the cloak against the neck edge of the hood. Sew together and cover the seam with a bias binding which extends sufficiently on either side to allow the cloak to be buttoned up.

With a pair of pliers bend the wire to make a little pair of spectacles. Place the spectacles on the nose with the side pieces pushed under the hair.

A tiny basket filled with coloured scraps completes Mother Earth.

Root children

Figure 18. Crocheted root child

Mother Earth's children sleep through the winter under the ground. She wakes them in the early spring. They set to work to make their new clothes as spring comes. Here we shall describe two ways of making the root children.

Crocheted root child (Figure 18)

MATERIALS
Brown knitting wool
Fleece wool, preferably brown
Brown or yellow mohair wool
A piece of thick knitted cotton 1 1/2 in x 1 1/2 in (4 x 4 cm)

METHOD
Make 3 chains, close to a ring and make 5 double-crochets. Next row make 8 double-crochets and increase each row by 3 double-crochets to make a little bag about 2 in (5 cm) long. Then crochet in back and forth rows over two thirds of the number of double-crochets to a total length of 2 3/4 in (7 cm). Finally crochet round all stitches decreasing less quickly until the head is closed up. Stuff the root child with wool. Close the

fleece wool in the opening with the piece of knitted cotton. Sew the mohair wool in loops round the face with sewing thread. Put a few stitches in the crocheted edge and in the piece of knitted cotton. In this way the cloth will sit evenly. Finally draw in the eyes with a pencil.

Sewn root child

MATERIALS
Fleece wool
A piece of soft thin knitted cotton 4 in x 4 in (10 x 10 cm)
A piece of skin-coloured thicker knitted cotton 2 1/4 in (6 cm) wide and 2 in (5 cm) long.
A scrap of thicker knitted cotton for the hands
A pipe-cleaner
A piece of dark brown material 7 in x 7 in (18 x 18 cm)
Wool for the hair
A tablespoon of rice

METHOD
Make a 2 3/4 in (7 cm) head with an eye line (see page 13). Cut out and sew the dress according to the pattern (Figure 19) and turn.

Bend in the pipe-cleaner at both ends so that the arm-piece measures 4 in (10 cm) long.

Wind some fleece wool round the pipe-cleaner. Draw the hands on a double thickness of material according to the pattern. Sew and turn the hands and slide them over the ends of the pipe-cleaner. Secure them on to the wrists.

Sew a tacking thread around the neck-opening of the dress. Fill the dress with the rice. Insert the neck into the neck-opening, pull the tacking thread tight, tucking the raw edge inwards. Spread out the pleats and set the dress firmly on to the neck.

Stick the arms through the sleeves behind the neck-piece. Gather the edges of the sleeves round the wrists and secure.

Embroider the hair (see page 17), colour the face and set the doll in the required posture.

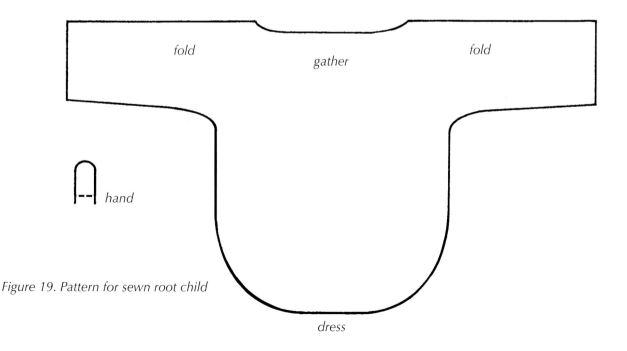

Figure 19. Pattern for sewn root child

fold   gather   fold

hand

dress

3. Spring

The coming of spring can be represented in a seasonal tableau in the form of the Spring Fairy spreading her mantle over the earth. King Winter leaves with his cloak of snow, and the dark earth takes on colour again. Spring shows itself particularly in the colours yellow and fresh green. Pink is also a spring colour, which one often sees in the buds of trees and shrubs, beneath which the green leaves are hidden.

It is nice to make the Spring Fairy out of silk, because it is such a fine material.

The Spring Fairy

MATERIALS
Fleece wool
A piece of thin knitted cotton 6 in x 6 in (15 x 15 cm)
A piece of skin-coloured thicker knitted cotton 3 1/4 in x 6 in (8.5 cm x 15 cm)
2 pieces of silk, one 18 in x 18 in (45 x 45 cm), the other 15 in x 15 in (38 x 38 cm)
Embroidery thread
A marble
Light yellow mohair wool or magic wool
FOR THE HEAD:
A card 6 1/4 in x 6 1/4 in (16 x 16 cm)
A piece of silk 7 in x 8 1/2 in (18 x 22 cm)
Bits of tissue paper in spring colours

METHOD
Make a 4 3/4 in (12 cm) head with an eye and chin line (see page 13). Let the knitted cotton project a long way down below the head, as it will form the body.

Hem the two pieces of silk. Laid over each other they make the gown. If the fairy is being made from two differently coloured pieces the darker should be the bigger and should be underneath.

Hem the silk with a thin needle and a silk thread — divided embroidery thread is suitable.

Fold each piece of cloth into four and form a little round hole in the middle by cutting off the thickest corner. Unfold the silk again and lay the cloths diagonally on top of each other so that the points of the uppermost (also the smaller) cloth lie at the centre of each edge of the bottom cloth. Tack with little stitches round the neck-hole. Push the knitted cotton for the fairy's body through, pull in the tacking thread and sew the silk on to the body at the neck.

The points of the uppermost cloth fall in the middle of the front, the middle of the back and on each side. Now the body can be filled with wool. Finally insert the marble and sew up the body. The marble ensures that the fairy hangs the right way up.

For the hair wind the mohair wool about fifty times round a book or a piece of cardboard about 4 1/4 in (11 cm) wide. Cut the wool through at one side. Lay the strands of wool on top of the head in such a way that they hang down evenly all round and sew them on with little back stitches evenly distributed, so that you get a parting.

Colour the face.

Now the Spring Fairy can be given some flowers for her hair or a proper fairy hat.

Cut the hat from thin card according to the pattern (Figure 20). Check that the hat will fit the head then stick the hat together. Cut out and fold the silk according to the diagram (Figure 21). Sew the oblique line with the raw edge inwards. Put the card hat inside and glue the raw edge firmly inside the card hat. Hem round the hanging material.

The wreath of flowers is made of little circles of tissue paper about 3/4 in (2 cm) diameter. Pinch each circle together in the middle. Thread them like beads on a thread with the needle always going through the pinched piece of the flower. Hang the wreath in the fairy's hair, round the hat or round her neck.

Let the fairy float in the air, suspending her by a thread that goes right through her hat, her head and her neck, and is fixed to her body.

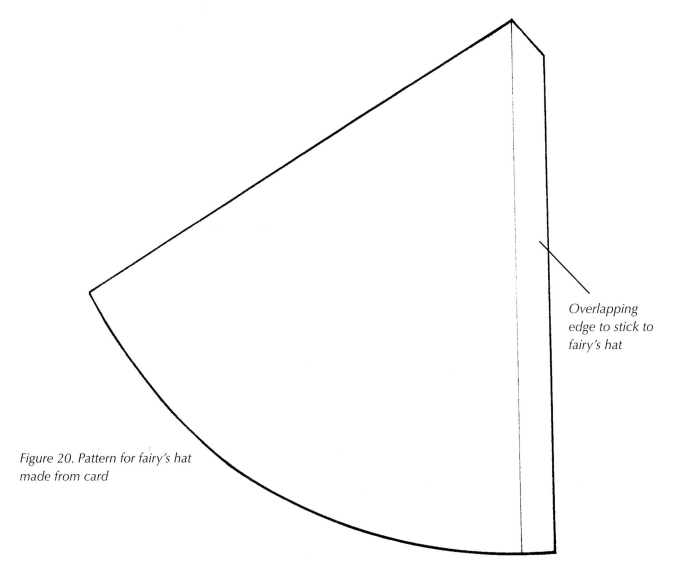

Overlapping edge to stick to fairy's hat

Figure 20. Pattern for fairy's hat made from card

Flower children

When the flower children come out from below the ground they are quite different in appearance from the root children under the earth. Each evening you can replace a root child with a flower child so that early spring comes into bloom. Following are a number of techniques for making flower children.

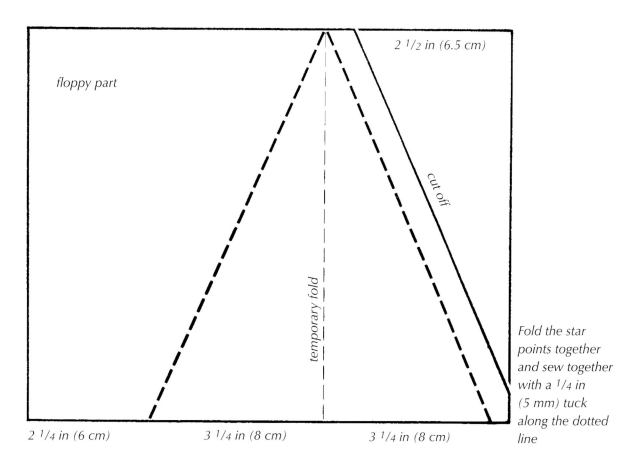

floppy part

2 1/2 in (6.5 cm)

cut off

temporary fold

Fold the star points together and sew together with a 1/4 in (5 mm) tuck along the dotted line

2 1/4 in (6 cm)   3 1/4 in (8 cm)   3 1/4 in (8 cm)

Figure 21. Pattern for silk part of fairy's hat

Hat and collar

Sometimes the flower children have a hat or collar of petals or green leaves.

As a pattern for petals and leaves use a real flower or an exact copy. Cut the leaves or petals on a strip (leaving them joined on one side of the strip, see Figure 22), or tack and gather them to get more depth in the flower. Such a strip can be fixed round the neck or pulled together to make a hat.

You can make a flat flower by cutting the petals out of a round piece of cloth. This is an alternative hat for some of the flower children. This simple method is more suitable if children are helping.

A flower hat can be finished off with a centre or a calyx with a little piece of stalk.

For the centre cut out a round or heart-shaped piece of cloth and stick it on the flower or sew it on with embroidery silk, which makes it look more realistic. You can also stuff a little wool under the centre to make it billow out.

For the stalk double a strip of felt and sew the edges together.

With some flowers the base is only a thickening on the end of the stalk. To achieve this effect roll a strip of felt about 1/2 in (1 cm) wide round the end of the stalk and sew on.

Sometimes the base is a calyx which is made in the same way as the flower calyx: tack a strip of felt and gather it. There are endless ways in which the cutting can be done (Figure 22). Make sure that the number of petals is right for the flower you are making.

A flower child made of teased sheep's wool

This is a very simple flower child which can be made by children.

MATERIALS
6 in (15 cm) teased sheep's wool pulled to the
   thickness of a finger
A strip of felt 2 1/4 in x 4 3/4 in (6 x 12 cm)
Scraps of felt for the petals
Embroidery thread

METHOD
Tie a knot in the middle of the piece of sheep's wool to make the doll's head. Choose one side for the face. Make a cloak by gathering the strip of felt along the longer side and fitting it around the wool doll, closing it round the neck. Sew a flower hat on to the head.

A knitted flower child

MATERIALS
Fine knitting cotton in the appropriate flower
   colour

Figure 22. Examples of petals for the flower children

2.5 mm knitting needles

Fleece wool

A piece of thicker knitted cotton 2 in x 2 in (5 x 5 cm)

A scrap of thicker knitted cotton for the hands

Wool for the hair

A pipe-cleaner

Scraps of felt for the hat, green combined with another colour

Embroidery thread in suitable colours

METHOD

Make a very simple 2 1/4 in (6 cm) head without wool in the neck.

The dress is knitted in one piece.

Cast on 14 stitches.

Knit in moss-stitch (1 plain, 1 purl on each needle alternately) for 24 rows.

Cast on 4 stitches at each end for the arms (22 stitches).

Over the centre 8 stitches knit one row plain, one row purl for 10 rows while continuing to knit the sleeves in moss-stitch.

In the next row cast off the centre 2 stitches loosely and in the following row cast them on again, forming the neck.

Continue for 10 rows.

Cast off 4 stitches at each end (14 stitches).

Knit 24 rows in moss-stitch.

Cast off.

Sew the arm and side seams. Insert the neck into the neck-hole and sew the dress on to the neck.

Bend in the pipe-cleaner at each end to make a length of 3 in (8 cm). Wind a little tuft of wool round the pipe-cleaner. Draw the hands according to the pattern (Figure 25) on a double thickness of material. Sew and turn the hands and draw them over the ends of the pipe-cleaner. Sew them on to the wrist. Push the arms along the

Figure 23. Flower child of teased sheep's wool

Figure 24. Knitted flower child

29

sleeve-openings behind the neck piece. Secure the sleeves at the wrists.

Stuff the doll from below with fleece wool so that it can stand up. Give the flower child a waist by tacking an embroidery thread through the line between the stocking-stitch and the moss-stitch.

Finish off the flower child by giving her hair and a hat or collar of petals (see Figures 23 and 24).

A crocheted flower child

MATERIALS

Fine knitting cotton
A suitable crochet-hook
Fleece wool
A piece of thicker knitted cotton 2 in x 2 in (5 x 5 cm)
A scrap of thicker knitted cotton for the hands
Wool for the hair
Scraps of felt for the petals

METHOD

Make a very simple 2 1/4 in (6 cm) head without wool in the neck (see page 13). The dress is crocheted from the top downwards.

Make 12 chains and close them to a ring with a half double-crochet. Work double-crochet on to this and increase 2 double-crochets in the next 5 rows, so that you have 22 double-crochets altogether. Continue crocheting till you have reached the required length (8 to 10 rows). Fasten off. Work the neck-piece into the neck-opening of the dress and secure it. Stuff the dress with fleece wool so that the doll can stand up. Make petals round the neck (see page 28).

For the cap make 3 chains, close to a ring and increase the next 3 rows by 5 double-crochets each time so that you have altogether 18 double-crochets. Make 5 more rows and fasten off. Put hair on the head and sew on the cap.

A flower child with a flower in her hand

MATERIALS

Fleece wool
A piece of soft thin knitted cotton 4 in x 4 in (10 x 10 cm)
A piece of pink thicker knitted cotton 4 3/4 in long and 2 1/4 in wide (12 x 6 cm)
A scrap of thicker knitted cotton for the hands
A pipe-cleaner
2 pieces of felt (green or the colour of the flower), one 4 3/4 in x 2 1/8 in (12 cm x 5.5 cm; the skirt) and 2 in x 3 1/2 in (9 x 5 cm; the top part)
Wool for the hair

METHOD

Make a 2 3/4 in (7 cm) head with an eye line (see page 13). Cut out the top part of the dress according to the pattern (Figure 25). Sew up the seams of the sleeves. Sew the centre back seam of the skirt and gather the top edge. Sew the skirt on to the top part, so that the centre back seams are aligned as are the centre front points. Bend in the ends of the pipe-cleaner so that the arm-piece is 4 in (10 cm) long. Wind some fleece wool round the pipe-cleaner. Draw the hands according to the pattern (Figure 25) on a double thickness of material. Sew and turn the hands and draw them over the ends of the pipe-cleaner. Secure them round the wrists.

Push the neck into the neck-opening.

Push the arms through the sleeves behind the neck-piece. Sew up the dress. You can also secure it at the neck and wrists. Stuff the skirt with wool so that it can stand up. Make the hair as described on page 16. Colour the face.

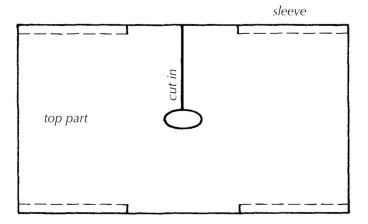

sleeve

top part

cut in

Figure 25. Pattern for flower child

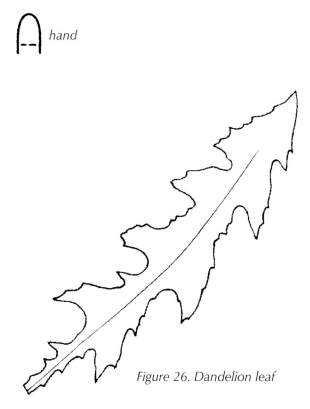

hand

Figure 26. Dandelion leaf

Felt dandelions

To make a felt flower, use a real flower or a drawing of one as a pattern. You can, of course, make other flowers than dandelions.

MATERIALS

Two green pipe-cleaners (or dye two white pipe-cleaners in green-coloured water)
2 pieces of felt in two close shades of yellow: the darker yellow 1 in x 3 in (2.5 x 8 cm) and the lighter yellow 1 in x 4 3/4 in (2.5 x 12 cm)
Green felt

METHOD

Cut into the yellow felt along the long side with the cuts very close together (about 1 mm). Take care as it is easy to spoil the felt while cutting in this way. Twist the darker strip first round the end of the pipe-cleaner. Fix it with a spot of glue or a few stitches. Then twist the second strip round it and secure this too.

From a strip of green felt make the base of the flower round the stalk underneath the yellow petals.

Cut the leaf as shown in the sketch (Figure 26) or copy a real dandelion leaf. Sew the second pipe-cleaner on to the leaf, as a central vein. Bend the leaf a little and the vein will come to the back.

Join the flower-stalk and the leaf stalk together underneath. The flower child can now hold the flower.

4. Easter

Easter brings longer hours of daylight to gladden our hearts, and in a sheltered spot the warmth of the sun can be felt once again. Spring flowers bring colour. The buds on the trees show that the leaves will soon emerge. The birds are singing and the lambs are skipping in the fields. Spring brings great joy and it is good to pause and consider this for a moment. Children happily engage with the new life, that which seemed dead but was not. For adults, nature reflects the resurrection, the true Easter festival. On the nature table you can represent this resurrection through garden cress, eggs, chicks, lambs and Easter hares.

Hen with chicks

Just imagine that you had never seen an egg. It looks like a stone and seems to be dead. How amazing, then, to see a little chick come creeping out of it. The chick represents new life.

Hen

MATERIALS
Crochet-hook No. 3
Suitable wool
Fleece wool
Red felt
Thick black thread

METHOD
Make 3 chains and close to a ring. Work 5 double-crochets into this chain. Into each double-crochet now work 2 double-crochets and continue until there are 20 double-crochets. Then work 1 double-crochet into each double-crochet (that is, once round the ring). Now work 2 double-crochets into the next 4 double-crochets and 1 double-crochet into the fifth double-crochet. Repeat 3 times (36 double-crochets). Then work 12 rows of double-crochets counting from the middle. For the neck crochet over 12 double-crochets continuously going round, that is not back and forth. The neck is 5 rows high. Now keep on working 2 double-crochets together until there are no stitches left.

Stuff the hen with wool and sew up the back. For the wings make 4 chains and then 3 double-crochets. Do not go back but continue to crochet along the bottom of the piece, 1 double-crochet in the base chain and 3 double-crochets in the other side of the chains. Then crochet twice more round, increase at the short sides so that the wing stays flat. Crochet the second wing in the same way. Sew on both wings to the sides of the hen's body with two stitches at the front. Make the eyes with knot-stitches (that is, make a little stitch, twist the thread a few times round the needle, pull through and fasten at the same place). Cut out a beak, a comb and two gills from the felt and sew them on to the right places.

Figure 27. Hen with chicks

Chicks

MATERIALS
3 mm knitting needles
Suitable wool
A thick black thread
Orange felt

METHOD
Cast on 20 stitches.
Knit garter stitch (all plain) for 3 rows.
On every following row knit the first two stitches together.
Continue until there are 4 stitches left.
Pass these 4 stitches on to a thread and sew the diagonal sides together.
Stuff the chick with fleece wool and sew up the bottom (or, if you leave the bottom open, you can put in a chocolate egg instead of the wool).
Give the chick eyes and a beak like the hen.

Hares

Traditionally hares belong to Easter because of their selfless way of life: it is said that when a hare is being hunted and grows tired, another hare will take over and run out in front of the hunters. According to another ancient tradition, the Easter Hare brings new seeds of life in the form of eggs.

A woolly hare

MATERIALS
Brown knitting wool
Brown felt
2 black beads

METHOD
The hare is made from three woolly balls.

Each ball is made from very short strands of wool bound together in the middle. The more strands, the better the ball. Catch a 10 in (25 cm) long strand between the ring finger and the middle finger of your left hand. With your right hand wind wool round the closed fingers of the left hand, holding the hand properly flat. When enough wool is fully wound on, tie up the middle with the loose strand which you have been holding in the left hand. Slide the whole thing carefully off your fingers. Cut open the loops. Shake out the ball and cut off any strands sticking out.

In the same way, make a ball over three fingers for the head and another over two fingers for the tail.

Sew the head on to the biggest woolly ball.

Cut the bottom flat so that the hare will stand up.

Sew the tail on as low down as possible. Cut out two ears from the felt and sew them on to the head. Sew the two beads on where the eyes should be and pull them into the head so far that they can just be seen in the fluff.

For bigger or smaller hares, use an adult's or a child's hand, or substitute a piece of cardboard.

Felt hare

MATERIALS
A piece of felt 5 1/2 in x 7 in (14 x 18 cm) the
   colour of a hare
A piece of pink felt
Fleece wool
2 black beads
Thin knitting wool for the tail

METHOD
Cut all the pattern parts out of felt, omitting seams (Figure 28). The whole animal is sewn together with button hole-stitch. Lay the two parts of the body on to each other and sew from the stuffing

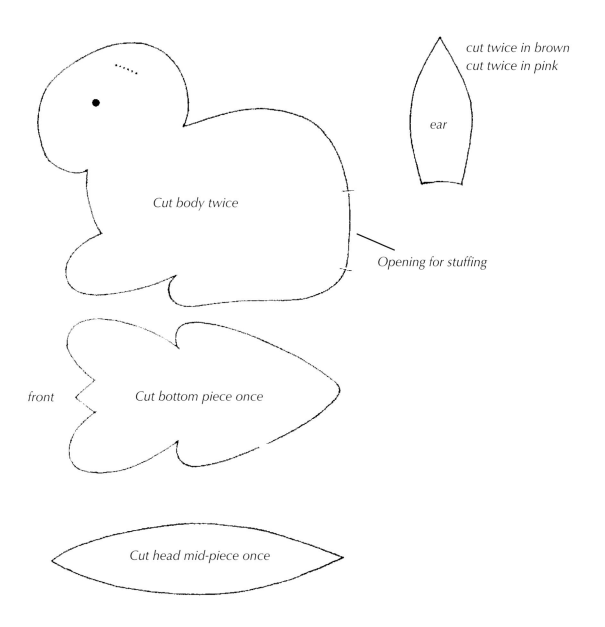

cut twice in brown
cut twice in pink

ear

Cut body twice

Opening for stuffing

front

Cut bottom piece once

Cut head mid-piece once

Figure 28. Pattern for a hare

opening along the back, to the neck. Sew the head mid-piece between the head-pieces. Sew a little piece under the chin up to the patch in front. Lay the bottom piece against the body and sew it on. Stuff the hare firmly with wool and sew up the opening. Button hole-stitch together a brown and a red ear. Fold the ear over lengthwise with the pink side in. Sew the bottom of the ear on to the head with the fold to the back. Make the second ear in the same way. Do not cut off the thread, but thrust the needle through the head to the place where the eye should be. Thread on a bead and push the needle through the head to the place of the other eye. Thread the second bead and push through to the first ear. Pull the thread tight so that the beads are lying in the material. Fasten off firmly where the ear was sewn on. If you wish, make some whiskers with embroidery silk.

Make a tiny ball of thin wool and sew it on for a tail.

Sheep with lambs

MATERIALS
White felt
Fleece wool
2 pipe-cleaners 2 3/4 in (7 cm) long
Tufts of good washed sheep's wool
2 small beads

METHOD
Cut out pattern parts for a sheep (Figures 29 and 30) omitting seams. Lay the leg mid-piece between the two parts of the sheep. Sew with button hole-stitch. Wind some fleece wool round the pipe-cleaners. Insert both ends of one pipe-cleaner into the forelegs and both ends of the other into the hind legs. Sew up from the breast

Figure 29. Pattern for a sheep (body and fleecy coat)

body part (cut twice)

fleecy coat

upwards over the head to point A. Join the head mid-piece left and right to point B. Now sew from point C to halfway down the back before finishing the ears. Stuff the head tightly with wool. Turn in the mid-piece at the back of the head to the dotted line D. Sew the dotted line D on to the sheep at point C. This makes the ears. Stuff the body and sew up. Lay a good tuft of fleece-wool on the sheep's back and sew it on here and there with little stitches. Repeat this until the sheep has a good fleece. Some sheep have woolly heads.

With a fine needle fasten a thread at the neck. Push the needle through to the eye socket. Thread on a bead and push through to the place of the other eye. Thread the second bead and push through back to the neck. Pull the thread so that the eyes are pulled slightly into the head. Fasten off securely. Work a few stitches for the mouth.

Instead of loose wool, you could give the sheep a coat of fleecy woollen fabric (Figure 29).

The photograph shows sheep in various positions. They are all made in the same way, but the lambs are smaller (Figure 31). They have a 2 in (5 cm) long pipe-cleaner and little or no wool sewn on.

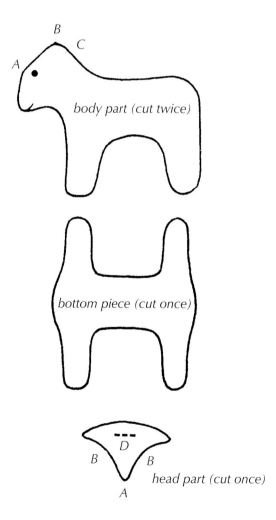

Figure 30. Pattern for a sheep (leg mid-piece and head mid-piece)

Figure 31. Pattern for a lamb

5. Ascension and Whitsun

Forty days after Easter comes Ascension Day. The flowers seem to reach to the sky, and the pollen even further. The buds are opening and the trees are turning green. The earth is full of life and nature is enticing us out of doors. New flowers appear on the banks and in the meadows. On the seasonal tableau, the flower children can constantly introduce new kinds of flowers.

Ten days after Ascension and fifty days after Easter is the festival of Whitsun. We suggest that at Whitsun the seasonal tableau be decorated with paper flowers. It may seem strange that just when nature is giving us so many flowers we use paper flowers, but the festival of Whitsun encourages us to work and to create. Paper is a material which lends itself well to this. We can be quite inventive with it and you will be amazed at your own ingenuity. You should not, in fact, be working from to a pattern, so we will only give basic guidelines.

Paper is not very durable, and certainly won't last in a sunny room. However, it is not a bad thing if the paper turns yellow. Next year, Whitsun will come again and with it, new inspiration.

Paper flowers

MATERIALS
Tissue paper or crêpe paper
Scissors, glue, sticky tape
Thin wire or wire thread
Cane, wire or twigs as stalks

METHOD
Winding on technique. Stick a strip of paper (which can be trimmed or not) firmly on to the top of the stalk with glue, sticky tape or wire. Turning the stalk creates a twisted flower. You can twist strips of contrasting colour and trim (for styles of trim, see page 28).

When twisting the paper, it can be pleated against the stalk giving more room to the calyx. The base of the flower can be fixed by winding wire or wire thread round it.

Pinching technique. Pinch a piece of paper in the middle and you will get a rough flower. Try out various shapes and sizes or different layers on top of each other. You can attach these flowers easily to the stalk with sticky tape or thin wire.

Pleating technique. Make a pile of little papers of one colour or complementary shades. You can also cut into the two sides facing each other. Fold the whole pile together like a concertina (Figure 32) and fasten it by passing a piece of wire round it and twisting it together. This wire can also make the stalk. Now very carefully lift the various layers upwards one by one.

Finishing off. These flowers can be stuck without stems on to a wreath which is made of green paper wrapped round itself. However if they going into a vase you should ensure that they have nice stems. Wrap them with a narrow strip of green paper, securing it with a spot of glue at the base. As you wind on you can glue on a leaf here and there. You could also use loose green sprigs as a basis for the bouquet.

Figure 32. Folding technique for petals

Whitsun doves

The white dove of peace is the messenger from heaven. Draw a beautiful dove yourself or use a pattern (Figure 33). Cut the body out of white card. Draw in an eye on each side. Make a little hole for the thread to hang it by and a slit for the wings.

The wings can be made of various kinds of material, such as a piece of tissue paper, thin silver card, thin white paper or a paper doily.

The wings are about 2 3/4 in x 5 in (7 x 13 cm). They are folded together like a concertina and inserted through the slit, extending equally on each side. Fan them out nicely. Hang the dove on a thread above the seasonal tableau.

The Whitsun couple

There is an old custom in the Netherlands that at Whitsun the Whitsun bride is decked with paper flowers and tinkling bells while standing under an arch adorned with flowers and greenery. The bridal party then processes through the village.

You can illustrate any of these customs on the seasonal tableau. We shall describe how to make the Whitsun couple.

The bride

MATERIALS
Fleece wool
A piece of thin knitted cotton 4 1/4 in x 4 1/4 in (11 x 11 cm)
A piece of thicker knitted cotton 2 1/4 in x 2 1/4 in (6 x 6 cm)
A scrap of thicker knitted cotton for the hands
Wire 2 ft (60 cm) long, 1/32 in (0.8 mm) thick

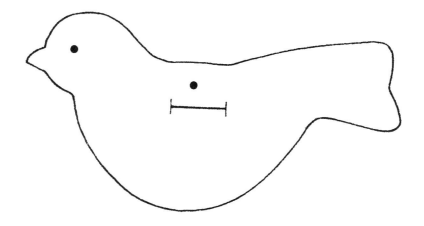

Figure 33. Pattern for the Whitsun dove

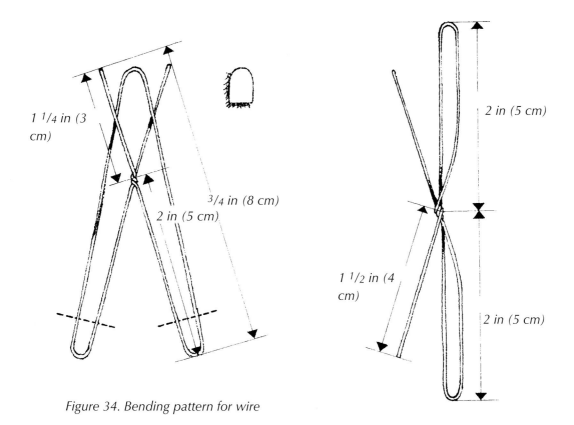

1 ¹/₄ in (3 cm)

³/₄ in (8 cm)

2 in (5 cm)

2 in (5 cm)

1 ¹/₂ in (4 cm)

2 in (5 cm)

Figure 34. Bending pattern for wire

The bridegroom

MATERIALS

Fleece wool

A piece of thin knitted cotton 4 1/4 in x 4 1/4 in (11 x 11 cm)

A piece of thicker knitted cotton 2 1/4 in x 2 1/4 in (6 x 6 cm)

A scrap of thicker knitted cotton for the hands

Wire 2 ft (60 cm) long, 1/32 in (0.8 mm) thick

8 ft (2.5 m) yellow mohair wool for the hair

A piece of white silk cloth for the shirt 4 1/4 in x 6 1/4 in (11 x 16 cm)

A bit of lace 4 3/4 in (12 cm) for the collar

Pieces of felt for the trousers and the hat about 3 in x 4 3/4 in (8 x 12 cm)

A scrap of silk for the stockings

2 bits of beeswax the size of a marble for the shoes

Bamboo skewers

Embroidery thread

Tiny bells or beads

METHOD

Make the frame of the bridegroom in the same way as that of the bride.

Cut out the shirt according to the pattern (Figure 35), allowing a small seam, and sew it. Gather the edge of the shirt's neck. Put the shirt on the doll and pull in the gathering thread, spread out the folds of the shirt and secure the neckband to the neck. Gather the cuffs turning the raw edges in, pull in the tacking thread and secure the sleeves to the wrists. Gather the lace collar and secure it to the neck.

The stockings are made by winding a piece of silk round the calves, turning the raw edges in on to the calves and securing with little stitches. Leave 1/2 in (1 cm) of the leg free at the bottom for the foot.

Cut out the felt trousers without seam allowance. Sew up the inside leg seams. Put the trousers on the bridegroom. Tuck the shirt in nicely. With a tuft of wool give him sideburns and sew up the central back seam. Gather the trousers at the waist and secure.

Bend the bottom of the wire of the legs 1/2 in (1 cm) to the front. Knead the wax until it is soft and form the shoes round the wire so that the stockings go into the shoes. Make sure that the soles are flat so that the bridegroom can stand up (Figure 36).

Cut out the felt hat according to the pattern (Figure 35) without seam allowance. Sew it together and put it on the head.

Make a bauble from a bamboo skewer with little bells on threads at the top. Sew the bauble on to the bridegroom's hand.

The archway of roses

MATERIALS

Wire 36 in (90 cm) long, 1/32 in (0.8 mm) thick

Green tissue paper 3/4 in (2 cm) wide and as long as possible

A number of roses without leaves and stem as described for the bride's bouquet

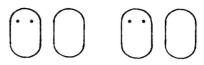

Figure 36. Feet of the Whitsun couple

Bend the two ends of the wire back to the middle to give a total length of 18 in (45 cm). Twist the wire together and make a nice arch. Make cuts into one side of the tissue paper along the whole length, each cut being a little more than halfway across. Lay the strip of paper with the cut side uppermost on to the wire and wind it spirally round the wire. Continue until the whole arch is covered.

Stick the roses on to the front of the arch. Bend the feet of the arch 3/4 in (2 cm) forward so that a pebble or stone can be balanced on them to make the arch stand up.

Figure 37. Roses made of tissue paper

45

6. St John's Tide

According to the calendar, summer begins when the days have ceased to grow longer. The sun is at its highest point. The trees are in full leaf. The flowers smell wonderful. Butterflies are fluttering around. Everything that was asleep in the earth during the winter has now emerged. All is green. Then comes the night of St John, the night when nature celebrates her festival and wonderful things happen — a midsummer night's dream. For a brief interlude, the sun entices us out of doors and lets us forget our everyday cares. However, imperceptibly we are moving towards autumn: the first fruits have already been gathered, and gradually the days grow shorter.

Beehive with bees

However far bees fly out to search for honey, they always return to the hive with their treasure.

Beehive

MATERIALS
A fluffy type of cord
A good reel of strong thread

METHOD
Make a little coil at the beginning of the cord. Sew it up. Pull in the coil tight to make it as small as possible. Make stitches over the coil to bind it together. Work on down the hanging cord, each time stitching it into the round of the coil which is already sewn on and, in this way, make a convex mat (Figure 38). When the hive is wide enough, work almost straight down to produce a hive like that shown in the photograph. Widen

the hive slightly at the bottom so that it will stand up firmly.

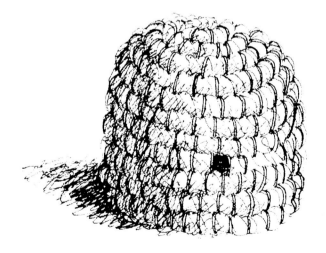

Figure 38. Beehive

Bees

MATERIALS
Catkins saved from the previous season
White tissue paper
Dark yellow knitting wool

METHOD
Make the bee's body by winding the wool about four times round the catkin. Cut off the ends of the wool and stuff them into the scales of the catkin. Cut the wings from tissue paper as in the pattern (Figure 39).

Lay the wings on to the body and tie a thread round them from which you can suspend them. The wings will now be drawn into the scales of the catkin. Spread them out carefully. Cut off the short end of the thread.

You can hang the bees on a ring of about 4 in (10 cm) diameter. Make the suspension threads of different lengths so that the whole thing looks like a swarm. Make some bees without suspension threads as well and pin them on or near the hive.

Figure 39. Bees' wings

Summer fairies

MATERIALS
12 in (30 cm) white well-teased sheep's wool
    ³/₄ in (2 cm) wide
4 ¹/₄ in (11 cm) white well-teased sheep's wool
    ³/₄ in (2 cm) wide
16 in (40 cm) ribbon
A piece of silk cloth 8 in x 4 ¹/₄ in (20 x 11 cm)

METHOD
Tie a knot in the middle of the 12 in (30 cm) teased sheep's wool and lay the ends together. The knot makes the head. Tie off the neck with the ribbon, tying the knot behind leaving the ends hanging. Lay the 4 ¹/₄ in (11 cm) wool (for the arms and wings) between the two strips of wool under the head. Cross both the left-hand and the right-hand ribbon over the chest. Cross them behind at the waist and then in front at the waist and finally tie a knot at the centre-back. Divide the cross-pieces into two pieces, the first for the arms. Moisten your fingers and twist the wool together to make the wrist. The second piece is for the wings which you fluff out well behind the arms. Fluff the skirt well out and let it come to a point.

Fold the piece of silk into four and in one cutting round off the four corners. Tack the cloth over the middle of the long side. Pull in the tacking thread until the pleats in the middle are ¹/₂ in (1 cm) wide all together. Sew the silk wings on to the fairy's back passing the thread up through the head so that the fairy can be suspended by it.

Grass

Long stalks of grass can be wonderful for decorating the nature table. See how many different kinds of flowering grasses you can find. They can be put in a vase as a bouquet, laid on the table or stuck into a potato (first make holes in the potato with a thick needle).

You can also plait long grass. Take three stalks or thin bundles and plait them together. The ends of the plait can be tied together with a flat knot, or bound together with another stalk to make a wreath. A wreath can be adorned with flowers inserted into it (Figure 40).

It is possible to make dolls out of grass. The best results are obtained when the grass is still moist. Take a bunch of grass as thick as your finger. Bend it double and tie it up with a stalk or a piece of string. The part tied off forms the head. The arms are formed by laying a thinner bunch of grass between the two bunches under the head. Tie round the waist. Make the hands by tying the arms at the wrists. The woman is now finished. A man is formed by tying off legs in the same way as the arms.

Figure 40. Wreath made of grass

7. Summer

During the summer holidays the seasonal tableau often receives much less attention. A cloth the colour of straw and fresh flowers are often all that is required. Beautiful things found by chance or something made by a child can be placed on the seasonal tableau. Even a dead bee can be put on the table to be examined and admired at close quarters, as can shells, pebbles, little sticks or mosses.

When the weather is wet or very hot it is pleasant to be indoors with children making things from treasures found outside. Here are some suggestions.

A mosaic of shells

A sand castle (add a little starch to the wet sand to make it stiffer, see Figure 41)

Little boats of bark and twigs with a leaf for a sail

A stick nicely carved with a knife

Little birds with feathers stuck into a body of beeswax or a fir cone.

Swans made of a pipe-cleaner with white feathers glued on and a beak of beeswax

A pond made of a glass plate with a blue cloth under it

During all the busy activities of the holidays, working at the seasonal tableau can be an oasis of peace.

Figure 41. Sand castle

8. Autumn

Summer draws to an end. As at Easter, day and night are again about the same length. After Easter the days were longer than the nights, and light had the upper hand. Then the plants and trees were growing; leaves and flowers emerged and fruit began to grow. Now it is time to consider what autumn brings. On to the seasonal tableau come fruit and seed. The tender rose of spring has ripened to a deep red and is now turning brown. As nature decays, we must have the courage to persevere. In order to strengthen this courage, we celebrate the festival of St Michael on September 29. Old pictures show the Archangel Michael fighting the dragon. He is also depicted holding scales. What Michael teaches us is to have the courage to stand our ground when nature is apparently dying, and to grapple with our own dragon-nature and to tame it.

You can create a dragon with chestnut husks (Figure 42) on the seasonal table; have the courage to take the whole prickly fruit, not just the smooth conkers.

A pumpkin child

MATERIALS

A piece of soft thin knitted cotton 4 3/4 in x 4 3/4 in (12 x 12 cm)

Fleece wool

A piece of thicker knitted cotton 2 1/4 in x 2 3/4 in (6 x 7 cm)

A round piece of orange flannel 7 in (18 cm) diameter

Orange knitting wool or magic wool for the hair

Figure 42. Dragon made of chestnut husks

Scraps of green felt 4 in x 1 in (10 x 2.5 cm) for the collar; 3 in x 3/8 in (8 x 1 cm) for the stalk

METHOD

Make a simple 3 1/2 in (9 cm) head (see page 13). With orange thread tack round 1/2 in (1 cm) from the edge of the round piece of flannel. Pull in the tacking thread a little, and stuff the pumpkin with fleece wool. Insert the neck into the opening and pull the tacking thread taut, turning the raw edge inwards. Spread out the folds so that the pumpkin becomes nicely rounded and secure the neck. Make embroidered hair (see page 16). Make the stalk by sewing the felt double along its length and sewing it on to the crown of the head. Make a little collar like the real collar of a shirt. Brown eyes suit this pumpkin child very well.

You can make all sorts of other fruit children in the same way.

Toadstools

MATERIALS
For a big and a little toadstool:
2 pieces of red felt 2 1/4 in (6 cm) and 3 in
   (8 cm) diameter (the caps)
2 pieces of beige felt of the same size as the red
   pieces
2 pieces of beige felt 1 1/2 in x 3 in (4 x 7 cm)
   and 2 1/4 in x 3 in (6 x 7 cm; the stalks)
A round piece of beige felt 3/4 in (2 cm) diameter (the feet pieces)
2 pieces of white felt 3 x 1 1/4 in (7 x 3 cm; the
   ring)
Various different and irregular pieces of white
   felt (the spots)
Little stones to fill the stalk
A piece of lead
Fleece wool

Figure 43. Toadstool

METHOD
Fold the felt for the stalk in half along the width
and sew it without a seam with thread of the
same colour as the felt. Close up the bottom with
the foot-piece. Place a flat piece of lead inside
at the bottom of the stalk. Fill the stalk with little
stones.

Cut out the circles of the red and beige cap-
pieces by eye so that they are not perfectly round,
and fold the beige cap-piece into four and cut out
a cross in the middle. Sew the red and the beige
layers on to each other and turn the cap through
the cut-out cross. Fill the cap lightly with fleece
wool. Sew the cap on to the stalk so that the cut-
out cross disappears. Cut the skirt-like ring into
points and sew it on to the stalk not quite at the
top (Figure 43). Spread the spots over the cap and
sew them on.

If the toadstools are to be little toadstool children, when you are sewing up the stalk leave a
little opening out of which a tiny face can peep
(Figure 43).

Teasel hedgehog

MATERIALS
A teasel (Latin *Dipsacus fullonum)*
3 pins with black heads

METHOD
Cut the stalk off the teasel leaving 1/4 in (5 mm)
for the nose. Cut away the long spiky parts round
the nose. Make the underside flat by cutting
off the spikes with a pair of scissors to stop the
hedgehog from rolling over. For the nose stick a
black-headed pin into the hollow opening of the

cut-off stalk (Figure 44). Stick the other two pins in obliquely above the nose for the eyes. The pins must be inserted right up to their heads into the teasel. If the hedgehog's spikes at the front are standing up too much, clip them off at an angle. The hedgehog should be pointed at the front and round at the back.

Hedgehogs do not like to be on their own!

Figure 44. Teasel hedgehog

Figure 45. Teasel spider

Teasel spider

You can easily make a spider from the long underneath spikes of a teasel. First cut off the stalk completely and then cut out the spider from the teasel (Figure 45).

A boy with a kite

The kite is sometimes a symbol of the dragon which makes it appropriate for the seasonal table at this time of year.

The boy

MATERIALS
Fleece wool
A piece of thin knitted cotton 4 $1/4$ in x 4 $1/4$ in (11 x 11 cm)
A piece of thicker knitted cotton 2 $1/4$ in x 2 $1/4$ in (6 x 6 cm)
A scrap of thicker knitted cotton for the hands
6 pipe-cleaners or 2 ft (60 cm) wire $1/32$ in (0.8 mm) thick
Wool for hair
2.5 mm knitting needles
A bit of matching red wool
Thin brown wool
A suitable crochet-hook
A piece of lead flashing
A scrap of felt for the shoes and the scarf

METHOD
Make a 2 $3/4$ in (7 cm) head with an eye line (see page 13) and make hair. The frame of the body is made from pipe-cleaners or wire.

Cut a piece of wire 12 $1/2$ in (32 cm) for the body and the legs, and a piece of wire 11 in (28 cm) for the arms.

Bend the wire frame as in Figure 34 (see page 41). Fix the arms to the body by winding the sticking out pieces of wire round the body. Wrap the skeleton thinly round with sheep's wool leaving 1/2 in (1 cm) of the lower part of the legs free for the feet.

The head can now be set in its place. Cut the knitted cotton of the neck-piece at both sides, as in Figure 35 (see page 43) and pull it down in front and behind. Tie it firmly under the arms. Fold the thicker knitted cotton for the hands in half. Draw the hands according to the pattern (Figure 35), sew them up, turn them inside out and draw them over the ends of the wire. Tie the hands firmly on to the wrists.

The trousers are crocheted sideways. Make 15 chains, use the first chain for turning. Work 14 double-crochets into this. Take again 1 chain for turning and work 14 double-crochets again. Repeat this until you have made 7 rows. Now make 6 double-crochets and 9 chains. Use the first chain to turn and work 14 double-crochets into the 8 chains and 6 double-crochets. Repeat this until 7 rows are completed and fasten off.

Fold the two sides to the middle and sew the inside leg up and then the centre-back seam. Tack a thread through the top of the trousers, put the trousers on to the doll, pull in the tacking-thread and so secure the trousers. The trousers come roughly under the arms leaving the feet about 1/2 in (1 cm) uncovered.

The pullover is knitted in one piece with stocking-stitch, that is one row plain, one row purl. These clothes are too small to require ribbing.

Cast on 15 stitches.
Knit 8 rows in stocking-stitch beginning with a purl row.
Cast on 9 stitches at each end for the sleeves.
Knit 8 rows.

Then cast off the 4 centre stitches.
In the next row cast the centre 4 stitches, but immediately insert the doll into the neck-opening. Finish the row.
Knit 8 rows.
Cast off 9 stitches at each end.
Knit 8 rows.
Cast off.

Knitting the doll like this is a little awkward but gives a very neat appearance.

Sew up the side seams and the sleeves. Secure the sleeves at the wrists.

Cut out 4 pieces of lead flashing (see page 13) for the feet as in Figure 36 (see page 44). Make two holes with a nail in each of two of the pieces. Make the shoes as follows: cut through the loop of wire at the foot and stick the two ends of the wire through the holes in the lead. This piece of lead then comes directly under the trouser leg. Bend the wires forward under the lead.

Roll the trouser leg up a bit. Lay the other piece of lead on the piece of felt. Lay them together under the foot, pull the felt well up round the leg, hold it fast there, wind a thread tightly round the ankle and up the leg until the felt is covered, then tie it tight. Roll the trouser leg down over the wound-up part of the shoe. (Do not use lead where there are small children, as lead is toxic if licked.)

Finally give the boy a tie from the strip of felt.

The kite

MATERIALS
Cocktail sticks, lengths 3 in, 2 1/4 in, 1 in (8, 5.5, 2.5 cm)
A piece of kite paper
Thread for the line

Figure 46. Kite

Lay the two longest cocktail sticks crosswise on each other. Tie the cross-point firmly. Make little notches at the ends of the sticks to take the stays. Wind the thread round from point to point, each time winding it round the stick into the notch to form the stay strings (Figure 46). Tie the beginning and the end together and cut off the ends. Lay the framework of the kite on the kite paper. Draw a line round the kite 1/4 in (5 mm) outside the stay string.

Cut out the kite paper, rounding off the corners. Stick the edges of the kite paper round the stay string. Thread a needle with 20 in (50 cm) of the thread. Pierce the kite paper at the cross-point. Draw the thread through the kite paper, unthread the needle and tie the end of the thread to the cross-point. Now wind the other end of the thread round half of the smallest cocktail stick to make the reel which the boy holds in his hand. Give the kite a tail about 4 in (10 cm) long to which little paper flowers can be tied.

The spider in her web

MATERIALS

4 pipe-cleaners 2 3/4 in (7 cm)
Some brown unspun sheep's wool
A fresh chestnut
7 wooden skewers or thin sticks about 10 in (25 cm) long
Silver-coloured embroidery thread

The spider. Wrap one end of the pipe-cleaner with sheep's wool: use a thin tuft of wool and lay it against the pipe-cleaner, hold it between your forefinger and your middle finger and twist it round the pipe-cleaner. Let go of the tuft, take hold of it again, pull it tight and make another turn round the pipe-cleaner and let go. Keep on working in this way until you have wrapped up one third of the leg. The trick is to keep taking hold of the tuft of wool between your fore and middle finger. As you let go each time the hairs of the wool can become intertwined with the padding of the pipe-cleaner.

Wrap all eight legs up in this way. Lay each pair of legs in a cross and twist them round each other once in the middle. Lay one cross on the other and bind around the middle with wool to make the spider's body. When the spider has been nicely stuffed you can still mark it with a cross of lighter coloured wool.

The web. Take a sharp knife and cut a little slanting notch every 1/2 in (1 cm) in the sticks. The top of the notches should slant towards the point of the stick. Stick the points of the sticks all round a chestnut which is lying flat. Tie the silver thread to the notch nearest the chestnut in one of the sticks. Take the thread to the next stick and wind it twice round in the first notch. Continue in this way until you have gone round all the sticks once. Then take the thread to the second notch and go round all the sticks once more. Proceed in this way until all the notches have been filled and the web is complete. Bend the spider's legs and put her in her web.

9. Halloween and Martinmas

Halloween, on October 31, is the night when witches and goblins lose their powers before All Saints' Day. The candles in turnips and pumpkins are like the last memory and afterglow of the summer sun.

A few days later, November 11, is St Martin's Day. Saint Martin was the saint who shared his cloak with a beggar. In some places the children go singing past the doors of the houses with home-made paper lanterns in the evening on St Martin's Day. The people then make the same gesture as St Martin did and give the children a portion of their harvest.

The paper lantern symbolizes the first glow of a kind of light which is new to the season: the first spark of an inner light which grows stronger as we head towards Christmas.

Lanterns

Turnip lantern

MATERIALS
A turnip, pumpkin, beetroot or swede
A sharp knife
An apple-corer
A spoon
A little pointed knife
A night light

METHOD
With a sharp knife cut off a cap from the turnip. If there are no particular marks on the rind you can make a little nick so that you can replace the cap in its right position.

Usually the bottom of the turnip is not level. To

Figure 47. Turnip lantern

make it stand on the seasonal tableau it can be either set in a ring or cut level.

Now we can start hollowing it out. With the apple-corer and the little knife loosen the inside of the turnip so that the pulp can be taken out with a spoon. It should be possible to manage with these three tools although the firmness of the turnip can vary considerably.

Once the middle has been removed work carefully towards the outside, pressing your other hand against the outside to gauge the thickness.

As you work hold the lantern up to the light occasionally to see if the wall is thin enough to let the light through. When the wall is nice and thin, you can cut out shapes in the skin, but be careful: cut into the skin of the turnip only, not right through the wall.

The cap of the turnip now becomes the lid, and it also can be hollowed out. An opening in the lid is necessary for ventilation. Place a night light or a candle in a metal container inside the lantern and replace the lid (Figure 47).

This lantern can be preserved a bit longer by immersing it in water occasionally.

A simple paper lantern

MATERIALS

A strip of thin cardboard 6 in x 16 in (15 x 40 cm)
Transparent paper (for example greaseproof paper)
Dried tree-leaves
A night light

METHOD

Cut or prick out one or more windows in the strip of cardboard. On the back stick a piece of transparent paper stuck with beautiful dried leaves. If the openings are nice shapes (as for instance a star shape) then transparent paper is sufficient. Stick the two ends of the cardboard together to make a cylinder and place it over the night light (Figure 48).

A tin lantern

MATERIALS

An empty tin with the top cleanly removed
Nails of various thicknesses, a hammer and a pencil
A wooden block
A night light

METHOD

Draw some designs on the tin. Punch out the designs by making holes with the nails. To preserve the shape of the tin while hammering in the nails you can put a wooden block inside. The light of this lantern shines through the holes (Figure 49).

Figure 48. Paper lantern

Figure 49. Tin lantern

Gnomes

Nature has often been depicted as having her special assistants: gnomes. At this time of the year the gnomes are busy preparing the earth for the winter, and so they are dressed in autumn colours. In other seasons a gnome can wear quite different colours.

Simple felt gnome

MATERIALS
Felt
Well-teased sheep's wool

METHOD
Fold the felt double and cut out the coat according to the pattern (Figure 50) without a seam allowance. Sew up the oblique side of the pointed cap. Run a gathering thread level with the neck. Stuff the gnome with a smooth tuft of wool. Draw in the gathering thread and join the coat together in front. To make the bottom flat so that the gnome will stand up properly, cut level any protruding wool.

Tailored felt gnome

MATERIALS
Fleece wool
A piece of knitted cotton 4 in x 4 in (10 x 10 cm)
A piece of beige thicker knitted cotton 2 $1/4$ in x 2 $1/4$ in (6 x 6 cm)
A scrap of thicker knitted cotton for the hands
2 pipe-cleaners or thin wire
Felt for the clothes and boots
A piece of lead flashing (see page 13)
A length of knitting wool
A tuft of coloured wool for the hair and beard

METHOD
Make a 2 $3/4$ in (7 cm) head with an eye line and a firm nose (see page 15). Bend in the two ends of a pipe-cleaner to make the arm-piece 4 in (10 cm) long.

Twist the middle of the other pipe-cleaner once all the way round the middle of the arm-piece. Cut into the material of the neck-piece at both sides. Set the head over the cross-point of the pipe-cleaners. Pull the knitted cotton down at the front and back and secure it firmly under the arms.

Double the knitted cotton and draw the hands according to the pattern. Sew them, cut them out with a small seam and turn them inside out. Push both hands on to the ends of the pipe-cleaner and tie them on securely above the wrist.

Cut out the clothes according to the pattern (Figure 51) with no seam allowance. Sew the trousers together with little whipping stitches. Put the trousers on the gnome and secure them under the arms. Sew on one shoulder of the smock. Put the smock on the gnome and sew it round the body and arms. Tie a thick strand of knitting wool round his waist as a belt.

For the feet cut out 4 oval pieces of lead (Figure 52). With a nail make a hole in two of the pieces. Stick one pipe-cleaner foot through the hole. Bend the pipe-cleaner under the lead foot, so that the foot comes $1/4$ in (5 mm) below the leg of the trousers. Make a loop in the end of the pipe-cleaner (cutting off a bit if it is too long). Now place the second piece of lead underneath, and pull a piece of knitted cotton or felt tightly round the foot, stretching the material, and hold it tightly to the leg. Wind a thick strand of wool round the ankle, tie it tight and cut it off in such a

Figure 50. Pattern for a simple gnome

sew up

fold

Figure 51. Pattern for felt gnome

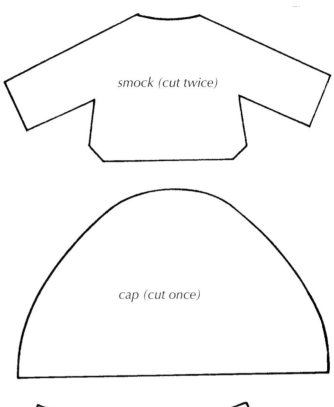

smock (cut twice)

cap (cut once)

Figure 52. Lead feet

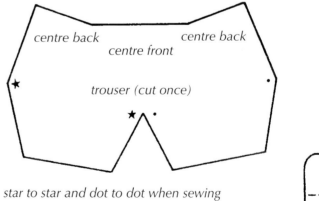

centre back   centre back
          centre front

trouser (cut once)

star to star and dot to dot when sewing

hand

way as to make a bootlace. The boot takes shape as you carefully cut off the bits sticking out round the trousers. Make the second boot in the same way.

The eyes and the mouth of the gnome are pulled in and coloured with a light brown crayon. Make hair with a tuft of unspun wool secured here and there. Make the beard by folding a tuft of wool double and securing the fold to the chin.

Sew up the cap. Sew it on to the head securely with little stitches (children will often pick him up by the cap).

A mouse

MATERIALS
A piece of grey felt
A piece of pink felt
Grey embroidery thread
Two little black beads
Fleece wool or rice

METHOD
Cut out the body-pieces from the grey felt. Cut out the underbelly and the ears from the pink felt according to the pattern (Figure 53). Sew the body-pieces together with little whipping stitches. Sew the underbelly part first to one side of the body with the pointed end to the front, and sew round the back. Stuff the mouse with fleece wool or rice then sew the other side of the belly on to the body. Fold the ear double and fasten it along the fold with a stitch, so that it bulges out a little bit. Sew the ear on to the place indicated on the head. Sew on the two beads for the eyes at the place indicated. This is done best by thrusting the needle through from the back to the eye socket. Secure at the place for the eye, thread the bead,

thrust through the head to the second eye socket, thread the second bead and secure, then thrust through the body again finally cutting off the two ends of the thread. In this way the ends of the thread are lost in the stuffing of the body and the mouse is finished off neatly.

Then comes the tail. Crochet a base chain 2 in (5 cm) long with unsplit embroidery cotton. Pull the thread through the last loop and sew the tail on.

A mouse is rarely alone …

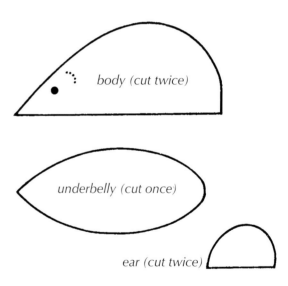

Figure 53. Pattern for a mouse

10. Advent

Advent is the time of year when we are preparing for Christmas. Advent literally means that which is coming. In order to create this mood of expectation, the seasonal tableau can be cleared and left completely empty. Only a blue covering indicates that something is coming.

There are various ways in which you can show that the birth of Jesus is steadily approaching: an Advent calendar, for example, with a door to be opened every day until the baby appears on Christmas Eve; Mary and Joseph could have a long journey around the room until they arrive at the stable at Christmas; or you could use an Advent wreath with four candles for the four Sundays of Advent (one candle is lit on the first Sunday of Advent, two on the second, and so on until all four are lit on the Sunday before Christmas, thus marking the passage of the Advent weeks).

During Advent we can reflect the changes on the earth on the seasonal tableau. In the first week we can put on some beautiful stones. In the second week moss, a fern and a little blossoming plant can be added. In the third week it is the turn of the animals: sheep, an ox and a donkey. On the fourth Sunday the shepherds appear on the fields, while Mary and Joseph make their way towards the stable.

An angel bringing the child can descend each day a little nearer to the earth.

Figure 54. Advent wreath

The angel

MATERIALS
White teased sheep's wool 14 in (36 cm) long
Gold thread 16 in (40 cm) long

METHOD
Take a piece of teased sheep's wool 10 in (25 cm) long and about 1 in (3 cm) wide. Tie a knot in the middle and lay the two ends beside each other. The knot forms the head. Tie the neck with the gold thread using the middle of the thread and making the knot behind.

Lay a piece of teased wool 4 in (11 cm) long and 1 in (3 cm) wide — for the arms and the wings — between the first two strips under the head. Cross both the left and the right gold threads over the breast. Cross again behind at the waist and again in front at the waist and tie a knot in the middle at the back. From the horizontal piece of wool divide one third for the arms and tie the wrist with gold thread 1 1/4 in (3.5 cm) from the body. Cut off the rest of the wool 1/4 in (0.5 cm) from the wrist. Fluff the wool lying behind the arms well out for the wings. Fluff the gown well out too.

During Advent you could show the angel carrying the child towards the earth. Sew the hands firmly together and lay the child in the angel's arms. After the birth, the arms can be spread out. Alternatively, the angel could have a staff, with a star in its hand or a star on its brow.

Saint Nicholas

St Nicholas' day is celebrated on December 6, the beginning of Advent. The great friend of children, St Nicholas visits children at night, and in their shoes, left out in anticipation, puts sweet things for the well-behaved or coal for the naughty. The celebration of this festival is great preparation for what is coming.

The image of St Nicholas which is presented to a young child can be very simple, leaving the details to their imagination.

MATERIALS
Teased sheep's wool 2 ft (60 cm)
A piece of red felt, 9 in x 6 in (23 x 15 cm; for the cloak)
Another piece of red felt 5 in x 2 3/4 in (13 x 7 cm; for the mitre — St Nicholas was a bishop)
Gold coloured embroidery thread
A round stick 7 in (18 cm) long, 1/4 in (5 mm) in diameter
A snippet of gold card
Gold paint if required

METHOD
Tie a knot in the middle of the wool. The knot makes the head. The two strips of wool form the body. Choose one side for the face. On this side pull out a tuft of wool one finger thick for the beard and tie the rest with thread immediately below the knot. Cut the beard to shape.

Cut out the cloak according to the pattern (Figure 55) without a seam allowance and sew up the shoulder seams to the edge of the neck. Tack along the edge of the neck, lay the cloak over St Nicholas' shoulders, gather it to a width of 1 1/4 in (3 cm) and sew it on.

Cut out and sew the mitre according to the pattern (centre of Figure 55) and embroider a cross on it with gold thread. Secure the mitre to the head with a few stitches.

Cut out the crook from gold card (Figure 56). Glue the tab at the base of the crook round the end of the stick and push the stick through the slits in the cloak.

Zwarte Piet

St Nicholas brings a reward for the good children, but in Holland he has a helper, Zwarte Piet, who brings appropriate rewards to the less well-behaved.

MATERIALS
A piece of strong card 5 1/2 in x 4 3/4 in (14 x 12 cm)
A strip of card 1 1/2 in (4 cm) wide
Knitting wool in brown, white and two jolly colours

METHOD
Wind the brown wool lengthwise round the strong card to the thickness of a finger, then carefully withdraw the card. Tie a thread round the bunch of wool a quarter of the way along its length. This forms the head.

To make the arms, wind one of the coloured wools round the width of the card, until it is half as thick as the body. Withdraw the card carefully. Divide the body into half, back and front. Place the arms between the front and back and tie a thread round the waist. Wind another coloured wool firmly round the wrists to a depth of $1/2$ in (1 cm) leaving $1/2$ in (1 cm) loops for the hands. Secure the ends under the wound-on wool and cut off. The feet are the same size as the hands. Wind round the bottom of the legs to a depth of $1 \ 1/4$ in (3 cm) and finish off as you did for the hands.

Wind the white wool for the collar length-wise round the 4 in (10 cm) card not too close together, then carefully withdraw the card. Lay the loose loops round the doll's neck and tie with a white thread. Fold the collar down. Wind coloured wool round the strip of card one finger thick. Withdraw the card carefully. Make a couple of turns with the end of the wool through the loops and form the wool into a turban-like bonnet. Place the bonnet on the head and sew it on firmly with wool.

Figure 55. Pattern for cloak and mitre of St Nicholas

sew up

fold

Figure 56. Crook for St Nicholas

The animals

Sheep

MATERIALS

2 pipe-cleaners 2 3/4 in (7 cm) for the legs
A pipe-cleaner 1 1/4 in (3 cm) for the ears
A pipe-cleaner 3 3/4 in (9.5 cm) for head, body
    and tail
Teased wool

METHOD

Wind fleece wool round the pipe-cleaners. Use a thin tuft of wool and lay it against the pipe-cleaner. Take the tuft firmly between your forefinger and your middle finger and twist it once round the pipe-cleaner. Let go of the tuft, then take it firmly again, pull it and twist it round the pipe-cleaner once again, let go, and continue in this way. This method works well if you take up the tuft of wool each time between your fore and middle finger, and let go each time so that the strands of the wool can become entwined in the padding of the pipe-cleaner and the strands interlock. It is important therefore to work with thin tufts of wool, while ensuring the wool does not just become a strand.

Begin the sheep at the head end. Lay the ear-piece on the longest pipe-cleaner 1 3/4 in (4.5 cm) from the end, and twist it round the wire to make the ears. Now wrap the nose round up to the ears (about 1/4 in, 5 mm thick). Wind round the ears from the top to the middle. Make the middle a bit thicker by winding the wool criss-cross here.

Now bend the head as follows: grip the first 1/2 in (1 cm) between your forefinger and thumb, make a kink and bend the point of the pipe-cleaner in the direction of the point where the ears sit on the head (Figure 57). Now wind over the bent part — the mouth remains free — and shape the head. Attach the leg part to the body 1/2 in (1 cm) behind the ears with a kink in the middle. Splay the legs out while you are winding on the wool. Start winding at the hoof, the legs becoming thicker as you proceed upwards. The hind legs are 1 1/2 in (3.5 cm) behind the forelegs. Once all four legs and the tail have been wound on, bend the legs down. Bend the upper part of each leg to the width of the body. The lower part of the legs remain straight. Wrap the body well to make it round and soft. Finally bend the tail to hang straight down.

Ox and donkey

MATERIALS FOR THE OX

8 1/4 in (21 cm) pipe-cleaner for the head, body
    and tail
2 pipe-cleaners 4 1/4 in (11 cm) long for the legs
A pipe-cleaner 2 1/4 in (6 cm) for the horns
A pipe-cleaner 2 3/4 in (7 cm) for the ears

MATERIALS FOR THE DONKEY
7 in (18 cm) pipe-cleaner for head, body and tail
2 pipe-cleaners 4 in (10 cm) for the legs
A pipe-cleaner 2 in (5 cm) for the ears
Teased wool the colour of ox and donkey

METHOD
Make the ox and donkey in the same way as the sheep although, of course, their posture is different. The ears are folded in loops. The pipe-cleaners should be bent according to the diagrams (Figures 58 and 59).

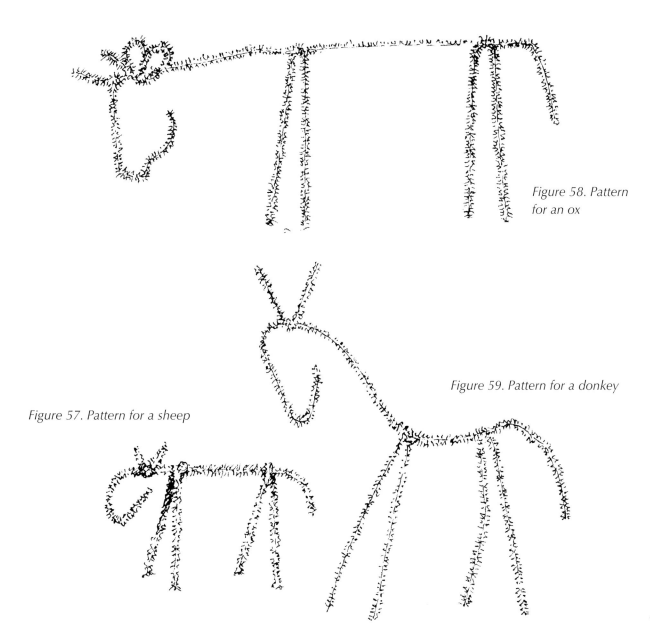

Figure 58. Pattern for an ox

Figure 59. Pattern for a donkey

Figure 57. Pattern for a sheep

71

11. Christmas

It is now the darkest time of the year. The days are short and the nights are long. The earth has turned in upon itself and appears bare and empty. Advent has made us ready, now it is Christmas. The winter solstice has passed and the days are going to lengthen, although the difference is as yet almost unnoticeable.

Our expectations have been fulfilled. To the seasonal tableau we can add red, the colour of life, to blue, the colour of expectation. These are the colours used for Mary's robe.

Crib figures

Mary, Joseph, the shepherds and the kings are all made according to a basic method.

MATERIALS
Fleece wool
A piece of thin knitted cotton 4 in x 4 in (10 x 10 cm)
A piece of skin-coloured thicker knitted cotton 2 1/4 in x 2 1/4 in (6 x 6 cm)
A scrap of thicker knitted cotton for the hands
Wool for the hair
A piece of soft card
A piece of cloth for the undergarment a bit bigger than the card
A pipe-cleaner
A piece of cloth for the sleeve-piece 4 1/4 in x 2 in (11 x 5 cm)
Cloth for the cloak
Glue

BASIC METHOD
Make a 2 3/4 in (7 cm) head (see page 13). For these crib figures, make simple heads with an eye line only. Draw in the eyes with a coloured pencil, do not make eye sockets.

The body is made from a card cone which is then covered in material. Cut out the card according to the pattern (Figure 60). Cut out the material for the undergarment rather larger than the card. Overlap the projecting edges to the back of the card and glue, so that no glue marks appear on the front. Insert the head by the neck into the opening of the card, having bent the card to a cone with a base of 2 1/4 in (6 cm). Staple or sew the two edges firmly together. Allow some glue to run into the cone between the card and the material of the neck and press the material firmly inside the cone.

Bend the pipe-cleaner in at both ends to make the arm-piece 4 1/4 in (11 cm) long. Draw the hands according to the pattern on a double thickness of material. Sew them, cut them out and turn. Push the hands on to the ends of the pipe-cleaner and secure at the wrists.

For the sleeves use either the material covering the card or the material of the cloak. Fold the material for the sleeves in half along its length and sew it along the long side to form a tube. Turn the sleeves inside out and push the pipe-cleaner with the hands on it through them. Secure the sleeves at the wrists; you can make a puff sleeve, a straight sleeve or a wide sleeve. A wide sleeve must be closed so that the construction is not revealed. Staple or sew the sleeve-piece on to the back 1/2 in (1 cm) below the neck. Finish the figure with a cloak, a sheepskin or a cap, hat or crown.

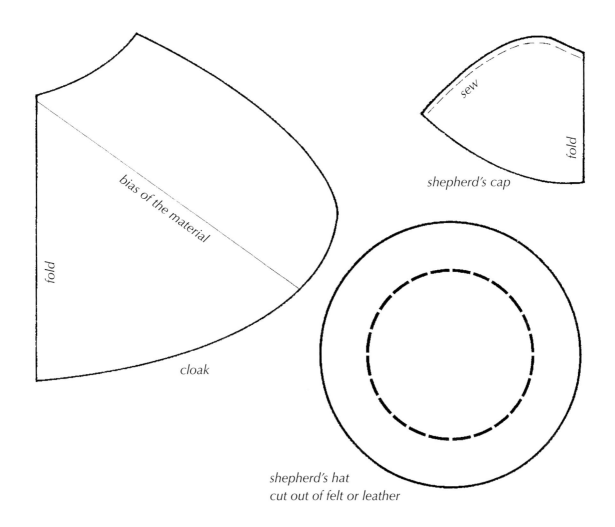

bias of the material

fold

cloak

sew

fold

shepherd's cap

shepherd's hat
cut out of felt or leather

Figure 61. Pattern for cloak, hat and cap of shepherds and kings

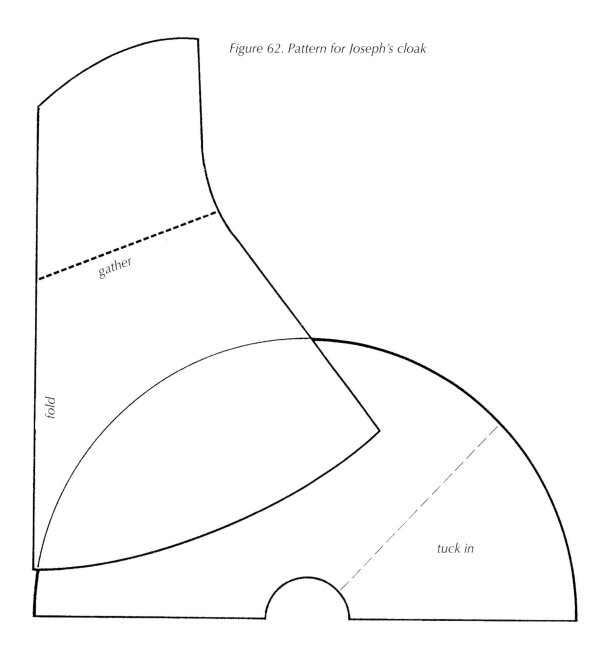

Figure 62. Pattern for Joseph's cloak

gather

fold

tuck in

Figure 60. Pattern for card cone body

The shepherds

Remember that shepherds' skin is probably weather beaten, their hair is rough, and they often have a beard which are easy to make by folding a tuft of wool over and sewing the folded edge to the chin. They are clad in simple materials, mostly brown in colour, but in any case use muted colours. Woven fabric and sacking are good materials for this.

The cloaks can each be different: for example a flowing cloak, made of a semi-circular piece 8 in (20 cm) in diameter. Fold the fringes in and secure round the neck, draping the cloak round the body. Hem superfluous material or glue it inside the cone. In this way the cloak can also serve as a cape. To make a proper coat, use the same material for the sleeves. The arms stick out through slits cut in the cloak level with the armpits. The cloak could even be a blanket loosely slung round, or an animal skin.

Make a cap or hat from knitted material, leather or felt (Figure 61).

The shepherd's crook can be a twig or the stem of a horse chestnut leaf. Glue or sew the crook on to the shepherd's hand.

A shepherd's bag is a strip of leather or material about 2 in x 3/4 in (5 x 2 cm) folded in half and stuck together with a shoulder strap stuck between.

The shepherds can appear in the seasonal tableau on the fourth Sunday of Advent, when their attention is entirely on their sheep. On Christmas morning they come to Mary, Joseph and the baby Jesus. Later they go back to their sheep.

Joseph

Joseph is distinguished from the shepherds by a smooth brown robe. The robe can be made in the same way as the shepherds' cloaks. Joseph's robe has a hood (Figure 62). Joseph also has a staff in his hand.

Mary

Mary has a bright red robe. She does not need any hair as her blue cloak fits exactly round her face. Cut out the cloak according to the pattern (Figure 65) from soft sky-blue material. Tack the u-shape according to the pattern but do not draw in the tacking thread yet. Lay the cloak with a little fold tight against the forehead at point A (Figure 64) and sew it on behind the neck. Bring the two folds at the side of the head down in front of the ears to meet under the chin. Pull the cloth up a bit at the centre-back by pulling in the tacking thread right to the neck and secure according to the sketch at point B. Drape the material round Mary, taking care that there is enough room for her to hold her child in her arms. The red robe remains visible in front. Secure the cloak at the wrists, again making a little fold. Hem the loosely hanging material with little stitches or fold the bottom edge in under the cone and glue it there.

The Child

Tie a knot in a piece of teased sheep's wool 1/4 in (0.5 cm) wide. Fold the wool double; the knot makes the head. Trim the body to a length of 1 in (2.5 cm). Arrange a piece of material 4 in x 4 in (10 x 10 cm; preferably pastel-coloured silk) around the head as described for Mary. Wrap the body up by folding the cloth in a cocoon shape measuring 1 ¼ in (3 cm). Sew the body with little stitches (Figure 63).

The three kings

On January 6 the magi, kings from distant lands, come to Mary, Joseph and the child. They have found their way to the stable by following the star. King Melchior, traditionally the first, has a red cloak and a grey beard. His gift is gold. King Balthazar, the eldest, has a blue cloak. His gift is frankincense. King Caspar is the third king. He has a green cloak and his gift is myrrh.

Each of the three kings has a white robe. Cut the mantles according to the pattern (Figure 61) using a rich material, for example velvet, felt or silk. Velvet is very thick and difficult to hem, so it is better to turn the edges under and stick them with some textile adhesive. Felt does not need to be hemmed. The cloaks can be trimmed with gold thread.

Figure 63. The child

The gifts can be represented by a little copper bell, a round bulgy button, a tiny coloured ball from the Christmas tree, a little box made of gold paper, a toy cup painted gold, gold painted acorns, alder cones or eucalyptus fruit.

Once the three wise kings have departed, Mary, Joseph and the baby Jesus set off on their way to Egypt, and so slowly disappear from the seasonal tableau.

The star which showed the way to the kings shines until February 2, Candlemas.

Figure 64. Mary's draped cloak

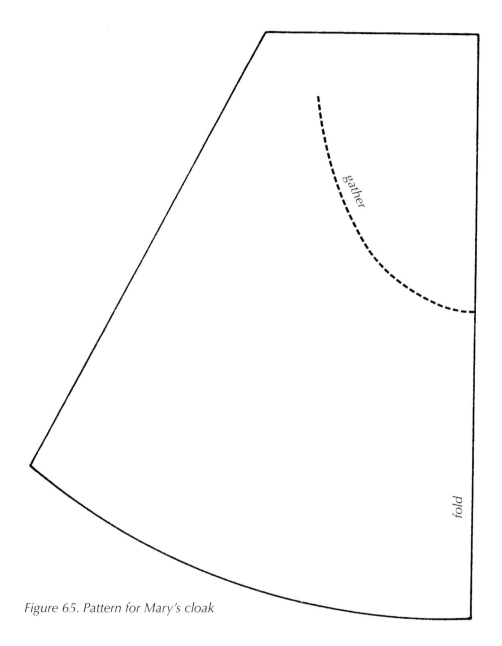

gather

fold

Figure 65. Pattern for Mary's cloak

12. Winter

When the snow comes and the earth is covered with a white mantle, it is clear that King Winter's rule has begun. Frost makes the air crisp and snowflakes come floating down like little crystalline stars. Children enjoy every moment out of doors, because before too long Mrs Thaw comes along with her broom to spoil the fun!

King Winter

MATERIALS

A piece of thin knitted cotton 6 in x 6 in (15 x 15 cm)

A piece of pale pink thicker knitted cotton 4 in x 3 1/4 in (10 cm x 8.5 cm)

A scrap of pale pink thicker knitted cotton for the hands

Fleece wool

A stand 6 in (15 cm) high (see page 12)

Wire 16 in (40 cm) long, 1/32 in (0.8 mm) thick

A piece of white or grey material 12 1/2 in x 8 3/4 in (32 x 22 cm) for the robe

A piece of white woolly material 16 in x 12 in (40 x 30 cm) for a cloak with a train, or a piece of felt 10 1/4 in x 6 in (26 x 15 cm) for a cloak with icicles

A round piece of material for the undergarment 10 1/2 in (26.5 cm) diameter

Carded unspun white wool for the hair

A piece of silver card 6 in x 2 in (15 x 5 cm)

A piece of silver paper 2 3/4 in x 2 in (7 x 5 cm)

METHOD

Make a 4 3/4 in (12 cm) doll's head (see page 13). Place the head on the stand and tie the scraps of material from the head tightly round the stand, using a thread. Push the thread through the hole so that the head is secure. Check the total height which should be 7 in (18 cm). Make the arms by bending the ends of the wire back to the middle. The arm-piece should be 7 in (18 cm) long. Sew the middle of the wire firmly to the back about 1/2 in (1 cm) below the head. Wrap the arms round with fleece wool to fill them out.

Draw the hands according to the pattern (Figure 66) on a double thickness of material. Sew them and turn them inside out, fix the hands on to the arm-pieces and secure them to the wrists.

Run a gathering thread along the undergarment 1/2 in (1 cm) from the edge. Place the stand on the centre of the material and gather the tacking thread. Secure the undergarment at the waist.

Cut out the robe according to the pattern (Figure 66) with a small hem allowance. Sew up the sides of the sleeves. Run a gathering thread round just below the neck, put the robe on King Winter, pull up the gathering thread round the neck turning the raw edge inside and secure the robe. Turn under a small hem for the sleeves and sew them round the wrists. Hem the robe.

Choose a cloak with a train or one with icicles. For the cloak with a train, cut a piece of cloth 12 in (30 cm) wide, round off the corners and hem. Cut out the cloak with icicles according to the pattern (Figure 67). Gather the top of both cloaks and secure them round the neck.

Now make the eyebrows, moustache and beard of ice. These are made of little tufts of unspun wool. Do not cut the tufts, but tease them out. This makes the hair more attractive. Fold the tufts over, hold them securely and sew them on.

To make the hair tease out a tuft of white wool about 8 in (20 cm) long. Place the middle of

fold

fold

crown

hand

continue to the required length

Figure 66. Pattern for King Winter's robe

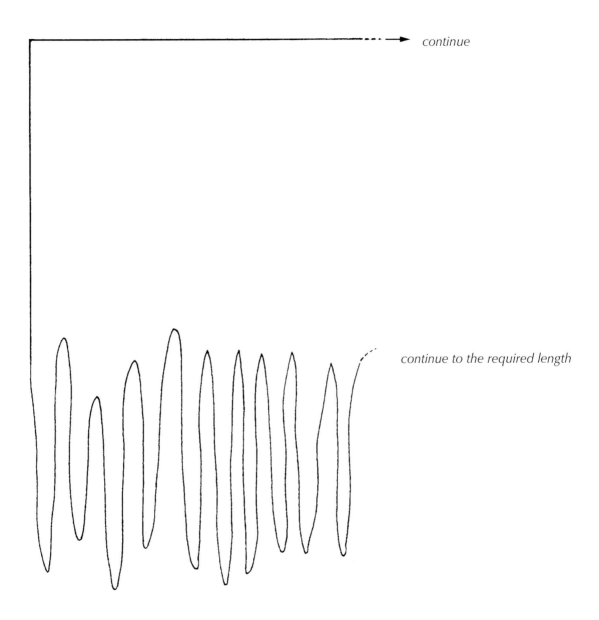

continue

continue to the required length

Figure 67. Pattern for King Winter's icicle cloak

83

this on top of the head and sew a parting with embroidery stitches on top only, so that the hair can easily be parted.

Cut out the crown according to the pattern (Figure 66) or according to your own design. Glue it together to fit the King and place it on his head.

Draw light blue eyes for the king.

His sceptre is a piece of silver paper rolled round a little stick. The stick can be removed afterwards. Sew the sceptre to his right hand. In his left hand King Winter holds the orb, a snow-ball made of a tightly-rolled sewn ball of wool.

Now King Winter can mount his throne.

Mrs Thaw

Whenever Mrs Thaw gets the chance, she will sweep the snow to one side. At first King Winter cannot be swept away as he simply snows every-thing under again. In the end, however, King Winter has to go back to the High North.

In spring Mrs Thaw sweeps all the snow and ice away. Wearing a clean apron, she wakes the Spring Fairy once again.

MATERIALS

Fleece wool

A piece of soft thin knitted cotton 6 in x 6 in (15 x 15 cm)

A piece of salmon-coloured thicker knitted cotton 4 in x 3 1/4 in (10 x 8.5 cm)

A scrap of thicker knitted cotton for the hands

A wooden stand 5 1/2 in (14 cm) high (see page 12)

Wire 16 in (40 cm) long, 1/32 in (0.8 mm) thick

Grey-brown knitting wool for the hair

Use grey colours for the clothing:

Blouse 8 3/4 in x 6 1/4 in (22 x 16 cm)

Skirt 15 in x 5 1/2 in (38 x 14 cm)

Apron 4 1/4 in x 4 1/4 in (11 x 11 cm) with a string 8 3/4 in x 1 1/4 in (22 x 3 cm)

Another apron in fresh colours:

A piece of cloth for the cloak 10 in x 5 in (25 x 13 cm)

A piece of cloth for the hood 6 1/4 in x 2 3/4 in (16 x 7 cm)

A press stud (popper)

A scrap of the same cloth as the cloak

A bit of beeswax (modelling wax) for the shoes

Twigs for the broom

A piece of fine fuse wire

METHOD

Make a 4 3/4 in (12 cm) head. Mrs Thaw can have lines round her mouth and a nose. Place the head on the stand and tie the scraps of material from the head to the stand with thread, running the thread through the hole in the stand so that the head is secure. Check the overall height which should be 7 in (18 cm).

Make the arm-pieces by bending back the ends of the wire to the middle so that the piece is 7 in (18 cm) long. Sew the middle of the wire firmly on to the back about 1/2 in (1 cm) below the head.

Wrap the arms round with fleece wool to fill them out.

Draw the hands according to the pattern (Figure 68) on a double thickness of material, sew them, Cut them out and turn them inside out.

Push the hands over the ends of the arm-pieces and secure them at the wrists.

Cut out the blouse according to the pattern (Figure 68) with a small seam allowance. Sew the blouse and cut open the centre-back. Gather the neck opening with a little hem right round, leaving the thread hanging. Put the blouse on Mrs Thaw, draw up the thread round the neck and fasten on. Sew up the centre-back. Fasten the gathered sleeves round the wrists.

Cut out the skirt and hem the bottom edge. Sew up the back and tack the top with a double thread, turning in the raw edge. Put the skirt on over the blouse, pulling up the tacking thread and secure.

Hem the apron along both sides and the bottom. Gather the top. Lay the mid-point of the string to the mid-point of the apron and sew it on along the top edge of the apron. Fold the top over the string and hem it. Make the second apron in the same way.

Make the hair from the knitting wool cut strands 9 $^1/_2$ in (24 cm) long, sufficient to cover the top of the head. Lay the wool over the top of the head, thread a needle with a length of wool work a parting with embroidery stitches. Let a few hairs hang untidily over her face. Make a bun at the back of her head by bringing the strands round to the back and twisting them. Secure the bun with a few stitches.

Hem the sides and bottom of the cloak. Gather the top edge. Hem a long edge of the hood to make the front. Fold the cloth widthways and sew up the back. Lay the gathered edge of the cloak to the neck of the hood and sew it on. Make a tab from a scrap of material, sew it on to the cloak under the chin and sew a press stud on to it. The cloak must be removed when spring comes.

Make a pair of sturdy shoes from modelling wax and stick them on to the front of the base of the stand.

The broom is made of a 6 in (15 cm) stick with various twigs measuring 3 in (7 cm). Fasten the twigs to the broom with wire and sew it into Mrs Thaw's hands.

Mrs Thaw sweeps the earth clean. Then Mother Earth wakes her root children who have been sleeping deep under the ground among the roots of the trees …

Figure 68. Pattern for Mrs Thaw's blouse

fold

fold

hand

Further reading

Activity and Craft Books

Adolphi, Sybille, *Making Fairy Tale Scenes*
—, *Making Flower Children*
—, *Making More Flower Children*
Berger, Petra, *Feltcraft*
Berger, Thomas, *The Christmas Craft Book*
Berger, Thomas & Petra, *Crafts through the Year*,
—, *The Gnome Craft Book*
Dhom, Christel, *The Advent Craft and Activity Book*
Fischer, Ute, *Weaving with Children*
Guéret, Frédérique, *Magical Window Stars*
Hörnecke, Alice, *Paper Folding with Children*
Jaffke, Freya, *Toymaking with Children*
Jaffke, Freya & Dagmar Schmidt, *Magic Wool*
Kraul, Walter, *Earth, Water, Fire and Air*
Kutsch, Irmgard, *Autumn Nature Activities for Children*
—, *Spring Nature Activities for Children*
—, *Summer Nature Activities for Children*
—, *Winter Nature Activities for Children*
Reinhard, Rotraud, *A Felt Farm*
Schäfer, Christine, *Magic Wool Fairies*
—, *Magic Wool Fruit Children*
—, *Magic Wool Mermaids, Fairies and Nymphs Through the Seasons*
Schmidt, Dagmar & Freya Jaffke, *Magic Wool*
Ulke, Viola, *Making a Nativity Scene*
Wolck-Gerche, Angelika, *Creative Felt*
—, *More Magic Wool*
—, *Papercraft*

Books for Parents and Teachers

Barz, Brigitte, *Festivals with Children*
Ellersiek, Wilma, *Nativity Plays for Children*
Jaffke, Freya, *Celebrating Festivals with Children*
—, *Work and Play in Early Childhood*
Masters, Brien, *The Waldorf Song Book*
Neuschütz, Karin, *Children's Creative Play*

Picture and Story Books

Beskow, Elsa, *Around the Year*
—, *Children of the Forest*
—, *The Flowers' Festival*
—, *Harvest Time*
—, *Ollie's Ski Trip*
—, *Peter in Blueberry Land*
—, *The Sun Egg*
—, *Woody, Hazel and Little Pip*
Muller, Gerda, *Autumn*
—, *Spring*
—, *Summer*
—, *Winter*
von Olfers, Sybille, *My First Root Children*
—, *The Story of the Root Children*
—, *The Story of the Snow Children*
—, *The Story of the Wind Children*
Thomas, Heather, *A Journey Through Time in Verse and Rhyme*

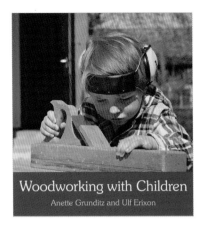

Woodworking with Children
Anette Grunditz and Ulf Erixon

A Felt Farm
Rotraud Reinhard

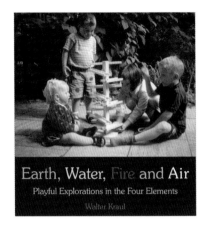

Earth, Water, Fire and Air
Playful Explorations in the Four Elements
Walter Kraul

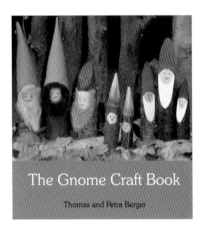

The Gnome Craft Book
Thomas and Petra Berger

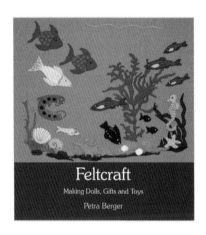

Feltcraft
Making Dolls, Gifts and Toys
Petra Berger

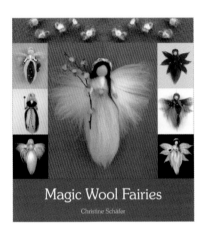

Magic Wool Fairies
Christine Schäfer

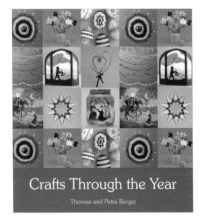

Crafts Through the Year
Thomas and Petra Berger

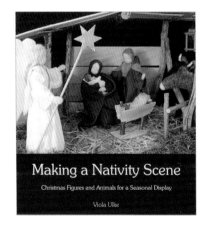

Making a Nativity Scene
Christmas Figures and Animals for a Seasonal Display
Viola Ulke

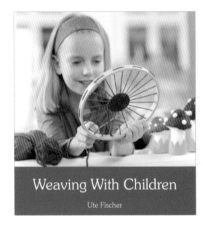

Weaving With Children
Ute Fischer

florisbooks.co.uk